CRITICAL TECHNOLOGY

For Patricia Ann Kirkpatrick, 1943-1996

Critical Technology
A Social Theory of Personal Computing

GRAEME KIRKPATRICK
University of Manchester, UK

ASHGATE

Published by
Ashgate Publishing Limited
Gower House
Croft Road
Aldershot
Hants GU11 3HR
England

Ashgate Publishing Company
Suite 420
101 Cherry Street
Burlington, VT 05401-4405
USA

Ashgate website: http://www.ashgate.com

British Library Cataloguing in Publication Data
Kirkpatrick, Graeme, 1963-
    Critical technology : a social theory of personal computing
    1. Microcomputers - Social aspects 2. Human-computer
    interaction 3. User interfaces (Computer systems) - Design
    I. Title
    303.4'834

Library of Congress Cataloging-in-Publication Data
Kirkpatrick, Graeme, 1963-
    Critical technology : a social theory of personal computing / by Graeme Kirkpatrick.
        p. cm.
    Includes bibliographical references and index.
    ISBN 0-7546-4009-4
    1. Information technology--Social aspects. 2. Human-computer interaction. 3.
Critical theory. I. Title.

    HM851.K56 2004
    303.48'33--dc22

                                            2004007711

ISBN 0 7546 4009 4

Printed and bound in Great Britain by MPG Books Ltd, Bodmin, Cornwall

Contents

Acknowledgements

Andrew Feenberg gave selflessly of his time and ideas to help me clarify the theoretical architecture of the book and I am particularly indebted to him. J.W.G. Wilson read the whole manuscript and provided many comments, some critical, all of them perceptive. Others helped in different ways at different points and this is the place to thank Helen Kennedy, Bo Kampmann Walther, Jon Dovey, John Armitage, Peter Wright, Michael Lavelle, Gordon Finlayson, Alan Carling, Chris Miles, Andrew McCulloch and Team CGS for their ideas, time and encouragement. Remaining faults with the work are, of course, entirely down to me.

Parts of some chapters have previously appeared in the journals *Max Weber Studies* (Chapter 2) and *Journal of Cultural Research* (Chapter 3) and sections are reproduced here by kind permission. A version of Chapter 4 was presented as a conference paper to audiences at 'Playing With the Future', a conference at the University of Manchester in April 2002, and to 'The Challenge of Computer Games' conference at the University of Łodz in August of the same year. Chapter 6 is based on a paper that was presented to the 'Power-Up' conference at University of West of England in Summer 2003 and to the annual game studies seminar at the University of Southern Denmark a few weeks later. I must thank the audiences at these events for their generous comments and criticisms.

Sarah Carling provided inspiration and adventure throughout the writing process. Natalia Hanley, Lynne Kirkpatrick, Christine Bisatt and Theodor Araby-Kirkpatrick gave solidarity and fun when I needed them. I am fortunate in having such friends and the book is for them. It is dedicated to the memory of my mother, who, along with my father, Jonty Kirkpatrick, always encouraged me to write.

Preface

This book is an academic text about a particular form of technology, but it is not a technical manual. Although it concerns interface design for the Personal Computer (PC), it is not a guide to 'good' interface design – there are already too many of those. To some extent, this book is a critique of the ideas that underpin much of that literature. It is well understood within computer science that the way computers are presented to people is a vitally important aspect of that discipline. Only machines and, in particular, programs that are appropriately presented will be efficiently used and become viable products. In order to get this right, there is now an established sub-discipline, named 'Human-Computer Interaction' (H-CI) that is given over to the analysis of how to make program interfaces that will facilitate the smooth integration of computers into the texture of everyday life for their intended users. H-CI is dominated, however, by established perspectives and paradigms in psychology, especially cognitivism. This means that program interfaces are being designed to work with a specific conception of the human as an individual and as a creature with a known set of capacities and endowments. The alternatives – interfaces for more than one person to use at a time; interfaces for people with 'non-standard' sensory configurations or other physical endowments – tend to be left out of the picture. The result is technology design that comports well with the expectations of a society that has been reared on 'personal computing' as the norm and which expects technology to come pre-packaged, mass marketed and attractive to its users. Anyone who is critical of that society and, in particular, of its tendency to wrap up human achievements as commodities for sale ought to be suspicious of this kind of technology design.

The book moves from this initial suspicion to develop a critique of the PC interface. That might seem like a perverse endeavour. PCs are, after all, associated with a revolutionary softening of the human experience of technology. Industrial machinery like cranes, rivets and production lines was brutal and its consequences, for the human beings who had to work with it, were frequently harsh and unpleasant. Computers may frustrate people but, repetitive strain injury aside, they do not place strenuous demands upon their physical systems. Indeed, one of the goals of interface design has, for some time, been to make computers 'user friendly' and pleasant to use. It must be acknowledged that the intentions of interface designers are more often than not benign and that H-CI is actually an unusually humanistic discipline within the scientific and technical context. In a way, however, this makes interface design even more susceptible to social critique. What does it mean when a whole layer of people within the sphere of technical design begin actively to consult Aristotle's poetics in their efforts to improve their work? When technology design is overtly informed by the need to create 'environments' that are 'pleasurable' and desirable for people to work in, then it enters into the realm of social and critical self-reflection. The humanities cannot service technology design with answers to its questions without also dragging technology and technologists into an engagement with their own concerns, which include the nature and meaning of pleasure, the importance of not finding things easy and the necessity of struggle in human affairs. Interface design becomes a field of controversy within the human sciences not simply because every arts professor has a PC on her desk but also because the way that machine was designed incorporates ideas drawn directly from her discipline. Until now this process has largely escaped the distinctive kind of philosophical mediation associated with critical theory of society. Interface design gurus have happily borrowed ideas of what people are like, about the nature of meaning and the desirability of some experiences over others, without encountering sustained resistance and debate from the disciplines that are centrally concerned with those questions. This book is an attempt to initiate that debate. In this, it is an intervention that tries to do what Habermas says philosophy must do in the current period, namely,

> ...to mediate interpretively between expert knowledge and an everyday practice in need of orientation. What remains for philosophy is an illuminating further of lifeworld processes of achieving self-understanding, processes that are related to totality. For the lifeworld must be defended against extreme alienation at the hands of the objectivating, the moralising *and* the aestheticising interventions of expert cultures. (1992b: 17-18, emphasis in original)

The point of what follows is to develop a philosophically grounded critique, or a sociological theorisation of the PC. This involves enlarging the scope of what is currently understood as the 'human factors' element in computer technology design. Rather than limiting our understanding of the context and consequences of a given design to the human individual and its 'normal' responses and behaviours, the critique argues for a more circumspect and sociologically sensitive approach.

The case of blind PC users, discussed by Goggin and Newell (2003), illustrates some of the reasons why such an approach may be useful. In the 1980s, when the first personal computers were made widely available, blind and visually impaired people were an important market segment. Using Braille and audio interfaces, many found that information processing was an area of economic activity that they could participate in as well as sighted people. Using a computer successfully at this time involved some understanding of data structures and required users to remember which operations were being performed simultaneously within, or even between, sessions with the computer. However, with the rise the graphical user interface, much of the cognitive burden of computing was shifted off the human user and what once had to be remembered became stored as a visual representation on the screen. The repertoire of command lines, easily converted into Braille, was replaced by 'dragging and dropping'; the manipulation of icons. In consequence of these changes, blind and visually impaired people were effectively disbarred from further participation in the PC revolution. As Goggin and Newell rightly point out, there was nothing inevitable or technologically determined in any of this. The rise of a certain kind of human-machine interface reflects the prior assumptions of a design community and the triumph of the needs and interests of some social groups over others. From the standpoint of critical social theory, this implicates technology design in the politics of hegemony, since each new artefact plays into a prior social situation, which it may reinforce or subvert. In this book it is argued that PC design reflects a range of social influences, in particular, the demand of the mass market for accessible standardised commodities. The alternative would be machines that were accessible to all, open to negotiation and revision and, perhaps, on occasion challenging.

The notion that interface design should include the values of openness and susceptibility to renegotiation and redefinition by affected people is, of course, inherently compatible with digital technology itself. Much has been made by theorists of the 'information age' of the flexibility that computerisation brings to various areas of human social life. If a commodity exists on planet earth then it can be found, purchased and delivered to your door using information processing techniques. Embedding digital technology in the environment is transforming a world that is inert, unresponsive and neutral into a place that responds to our needs and even answers our questions. Digital technology posits a logic of human empowerment and enhanced control for individuals, rather than one of standardisation, seriality and inertia. It is clear that where the latter tendencies are present in our experience with those technologies, there something strange is going on. To understand why so much of our experience with computers is frustrating; why so many of the reports we read about networked computing involve frightening 'hackers', and why we still associate computers with the controlling hand of the police state, we need to understand how the inherently liberating potential of digital technology has been corrupted and stymied by a specific social system. Digital technology has the potential to be life-enhancing and empowering, but under social conditions dominated by the needs of unregulated capitalism its development is thwarted.

This book examines this process at three levels. First, it attempts to bring to light the assumptions that are sedimented in current interface design principles. As just indicated, these have been thematised with deliberate reference to humanities ideas by visionaries within the field of interface design. The argument presented here places these ideas in their historical and social context, showing how ideas that can seem quite radical in one context can take on quite a different aspect when redeployed in different circumstances. Hence, in chapter two I discuss the radical aspirations of the hippy hackers who invented the PC and who saw in it a kind of paradigm for democracy through the equal empowerment of each individual computer user. This idea becomes distorted and subject to an ironic reversal as the PC becomes both socially ubiquitous and redesigned to inhibit user experimentation. Similarly, in chapter three I investigate the aesthetics of PC interface design and find that notions concerning form and function, and established associations between naturalist modernism and human emancipation become more fraught in the context of PC design. In particular, the integration of the technical and the pleasurable, of the human and the natural-physical, can be done in a way that inhibits the development of technical understanding.

At the same time as it engages the issue of which humanistic principles can and ought to inform technology design, the argument presented here also challenges established conceptions of the technical within the humanities. In particular, critical theory has for too long aligned technical reason and the activities of technologists with instrumental reason. The latter is that way of approaching the world that would subordinate everything to human control, giving us ever more leverage over things while blinding us to other ways of appreciating them and to the consequences of our dominion over them. In chapter one I join forces with Andrew Feenberg in trying to subvert this vision. Technologists and technological reason are neutral with respect to social systems based on super-exploitation of nature and the patterns of domination and violence associated with capitalism. It is in the social processes that shape and use technology that we need to identify distortions of what is, I argue, a natural human desire to experiment with and gain mastery of objects in the physical world. In chapter one I try to go beyond Feenberg's thought on these issues, to decompose the notion of instrumental reason into those parts which are anthropologically given – a necessary part of the repertoire of the human creature – and those which are overdeveloped; distorted by life in societies where the drive to control becomes pathological. Explicitly naturalising the human desire to technologise bits of reality becomes the basis for my suggestion, in chapter five, that hacking a computer is a natural activity. The criminalisation of hacking and its conversion into something dangerous and menacing is an effect of the social construction that this society puts on computing as a socio-technical practice. It is nothing to do with an alleged defect in the 'hacker'.

The third level of mediation in between the technological and cultural levels of personal computing that the reader will find here, concerns the notion of a technical politics. I have developed Feenberg's idea that competing social forces may tactically renegotiate the role machines play in their working lives. The uniquely open character of the PC; the fact that its function has not been, and probably cannot be finally pinned down, means that its design remains contested on a daily basis even though it is a mass commodity. Drawing on Feenberg and Beck's notion of a 'reflexive politicisation' of the technical basis of contemporary social life, I argue that how we react to the machine and the kinds of thing we get it to do have implications for the future of the technology and, therefore, for the future character of society. I theorise this in terms of computational temperaments; in particular, I oppose the disposition of the computer hacker to that of the computer game player.

In this book the idea of the hacker is used in two different ways. In chapter two, the hackers are those unusual people at MIT in the 1960s and in small informal computer clubs in the US in the following decade. Here the term denotes a specific sub-set of the population who were exposed to the computer and found themselves drawn to it. Later chapters use the term in a different sense. In chapter five, in particular, the hacker is a ideal typical representation of a certain way of reacting to the computer, after it has been subject to three or four generations of social construction and, especially, after the interface has become a major part of the machine. Continuous between the two uses is the idea of intense, focused engagement with the machine at levels that are deliberately obscured by contemporary interface design. Hacking as an activity has a continuous history and it entails a certain temperamental disposition towards the machine. What has changed is that it no longer makes much sense to ascribe this temperament to a narrow sub-group. Everyone hacks in the sense just described, because the friendly interface never deceives anyone for too long. We all oscillate between the hacking temperament and the mind-set of the user, who simply plays along with the interface cues and accepts the string of metaphors thrown out at her as if they constituted a meaningful narration of her day's work. The user too is an ideal typical construct, this time projected by the hegemonic interface design community. A good user is a conformist, who finds the world provided for her at the interface quite seamless and satisfactory. This frame of mind is, again, all of us at certain periods in our use of a PC. I argue in chapter four that this temperament finds its highest expression in the computer gamer.

The point of identifying and labelling computational temperaments in this way is that they provide insight into the politics of PC use and, especially, they put the spotlight on the political function of the hegemonic interface. The primary political role of friendly interfaces has been to police who can know what about the PC and what it is really doing. The computer gamer is like the ideal consumer who rests content with what she can buy from the system and is not curious to know more. In contrast, when we assume the standpoint of the hacker we become adolescent rebels, raging against the machine as it is presented to us and demanding transparency. These conflicting temperaments need to be understood in terms of the central importance of education and learning to contemporary social development. In so far as it speaks to the interface design community, this book is a call for interfaces that calibrate the need to provide programs that enable people to do things unrelated to computing with the principle that they should know what, in computing terms, they are doing when they use the program. Interfaces should be designed to allow program users to understand as much of what is going on as they want to. This conflicts with current capitalist priorities concerning ownership of code and so on. However, the current emphasis on concealment of the coding and technical levels behind a veneer of metaphor and simulation runs to ground on even more fundamental aspects of the socio-technical situation – the metaphors break down, people naturally want to know how their machines really work.

The technical politics advocated here concerns more than those who have a direct interest in interface design, however. The boundary between interface designer and interface user has been socially constructed and remains vulnerable to various kinds of transgression. In this context there are a range of questions that are likely to become more sociologically significant and which can only be properly answered by communities of well-informed people working with experts. At present, for example, corporations dictate that it is acceptable for the manufacturer of your operating system to periodically 'steer' your machine towards their web-site to implant what they describe as 'software updates'. It is not acceptable for a group of hackers to hijack your machine and perform essentially the same operation. Corporations and lawyers are determining the technical circumstances under which an e-mail is a legally binding document. And, as I write this on a screen of light real money is changing hands for the exchange of 'virtual' objects, such as on-line game characters with special powers. In these activities and others we are collectively shaping a new social order in which the networked PC plays a decisive role. In these activities the material basis of social life in the future is being moulded to the needs of money and power. The two temperaments – hacking and gaming – represent possible responses to this. One way forward is openly subversive. Hacking denies the validity of any agreement on the materiality of virtual objects, the normative validity of conventions established around web use and the legality of property claims over data. A gaming mentality, in contrast, constitutes a kind of resignation to a cyber-future that has been shaped behind our backs. In our technical politics we need to re-integrate these two temperamental dispositions and develop a realistic and pragmatic politics that can exploit the critical possibilities opened up by digital technology. On this basis the PC can retain its status as critical technology.

Chapter 1

What Does Critical Theory Criticise About Technology?

Introduction

In this chapter I attempt to clarify a theoretical basis for social critique of contemporary technology. Marxism tends to view technology as the explanatory basis of social change rather than as a social variable itself waiting to be explained by historical development. Progress in the technological base leads to quantitative shifts in production which can themselves only be achieved through social reorganisation. This in turn drives alterations in the way that people think about themselves, each other and the world. All these changes are caused by, or explained functionally with reference to technology, while changes in technology itself are outside the compass of social explanation. This is a positivistic view and, to be fair, we normally find its full-blown version only in caricatures of the Marxist position.[1]

Within the same, critical tradition as Marxism, Frankfurt School theorists offered a romantic indictment of technology. In this critique, technology is an outgrowth of the negative features of modernity (Adorno and Horkheimer 1992). An egoistic, paranoid and hostile reason attacks the world looking for patterns that will afford opportunities for leverage and enhance the success of future actions. These it exploits, turning observed regularities to its own advantage through knowing interventions. This instrumental orientation is oblivious to everything that does not reflect its own drive to control right back at it. Considerations of meaning and value are gradually deleted from the repertoire of human concerns and technology begets more technology. The technical-instrumentalist attitude grows more diffuse and reinforces capitalist social relations and processes, providing domination to accompany exploitation.

Both these approaches neglect the possibility that technology may be implicated in social conflicts in more complex, multivalent ways. They also overlook the possibility that technical development may be subject to willed transformations for good or ill.[2] Technology is neither beyond the scope of social critique nor simply a product of negative social developments. It is present within the field of social relations, contested – susceptible to being pushed as well as

---

[1] Although Cohen (1978) provides a robust defence of this kind of interpretation.

[2] This idea is, however, present in some later Frankfurt School work (See Marcuse 1964).

pushing. In the work of Andrew Feenberg, contemporary critical theory has begun to address this hitherto neglected possibility. Drawing on a range of intellectual sources Feenberg has developed a sophisticated framework with which to answer the question in the title of the current chapter. By subjecting his work to critical scrutiny here I hope to clarify the conceptual basis for the social critique of personal computing and of the PC interface that is developed in subsequent chapters.

On Feenberg's reading of Marx, we find there remarks suggesting three plausible lines of social criticism of technology:

1. Technologies can be negative in themselves in that they are designed simply to do bad, stupid things. An example of this, perhaps not uncontroversial, would be weapons of mass destruction. These things produce mass anxiety or, if used, mass death.[3] A less controversial example would be the use of machinery to produce plastic replicas of Elvis Presley, which are completely useless. Feenberg, in his discussion of Marx, calls this the 'product critique'.

2. Technology can be used badly, so that productive benefits are gained at the expense of, or at least without due care for, the well-being of human operatives. The production line would be an obvious illustration of this, which Feenberg calls the 'process critique' of technology.

3. Technology can be designed and produced in ways that systematically reflect and embody the interests of some groups in society and systematically neglect and exclude the interests of others. This perspective has some grounding in Marx, but is really Feenberg's own innovation. Here he draws on the relatively new discipline of 'technology studies' to insist that social forces routinely shape technology at various points in its development. Articulating this to critical theory's conception of capitalist society as subject to an unjustifiable power differential, he has established a new perspective on the relationship between capitalist society and contemporary technology.

The social shaping of technology can be illustrated with reference to any number of examples highlighting the ways in which various social actors and groups have perceived different, sometimes conflicting potentials within identical technical objects. Feenberg gives the example of the bicycle. Initially received as a sports vehicle which people could use to race one another, its early instantiations had large front wheels. This made them fast but ungainly. As more people perceived them as ways to get around, bicycles were redesigned to have more regular wheels and, ultimately, redefined as a leisure and transportation device, with racing as a minority pursuit. In this way, the technical object – frame, wheels, handlebars – was subjected to social redefinition before emerging into the light of day as the mundane object we try to avoid crashing into when driving our cars. The point of this and other constructionist fables is that the technology did not contain an

---

[3] The controversy would be that they have also been used to secure world peace and to 'win' the Cold War.

immanent logic that pointed from the wheel to the bicycle, with cyclists as unwitting recipients of the cycling experience. The whole notion of cycling was formed in a social context and the technical object was forged in the heat generated by this context.

Although he has incorporated the insights of social constructionism, Feenberg has not accepted the relativism implicit in that approach when taken to its extremes. Technology is shaped by social forces and changes but it is still always technology and, as such, it is more than the sum of its social relations. There is a reason for taking the invention of the bicycle to be primarily a technological event rather than an artistic or cultural one. Feenberg's goal is to develop a critical theory of technology that evades the positivism that puts technology outside of social processes and changes, while at the same time it must avoid lapsing into a relativism that sees each technological artefact simply in terms of its own, local, social history. As Feenberg points out, the latter would detach the story of technological changes entirely from the larger narrative of which they are an integral part, namely, 'philosophical reflection on modernity' (1999:201).

What Is 'Technology'?

It is impossible to provide an abstract definition of 'technology'. As Feenberg puts it, '...there is no such thing as technology "in itself" since technologies exist as such only in the context of one or another sort of employment' (1991:31) Yet, as just stated, there must be something that these employments have in common, defining them all as instances of technology and situating them within the problematics of modernity. This essence of technology consists in recurrent patterns, clusters of social variables that are suggestive of a certain kind of continuous presence. Feenberg proposes,

> ...a radical redefinition of technology that crosses the usual line between artefacts and social relations assumed by common sense and philosophers alike... I will define the essence of technology as the *systematic* locus for the sociocultural variables that actually diversify its historical realization. (1999: 201)

In capitalist society non-technologists encounter technical objects only after they have been codified as such. This is how people know what they are and how to respond to them appropriately. We want to say that there is an essence of technology that precedes all such codifications, but such a thing is impossible: All human experiences of technology have been codified in ways that reflect parallel systems of social organisation and culture. The commonality we seek must be located here, at the level of patterns of organisation and human orientation.

If the technological is constituted in and through actions and attitudes themselves manifest as socio-cultural variables then it can be things, or people, or situations, or processes. The definitive point would be the orientation that people had to the thing; its capacity to attract the right (technical) kind of attention. For reasons to be presented shortly, I think this definition marks an important advance for critical theory of technology. However, it should be noted that it sits uncomfortably with some of Feenberg's other remarks, where it seems that 'technology' denotes a specific class of objects – the common sense definition, if you like. In particular, Feenberg suggests that technology be considered a steering medium, like money or power in Habermas's system. That is to say, that technology controls social integration processes, obliging us to act in ways that comport with systemic requirements. However, technology cannot be defined as broadly as it is in the radical redefinition and be a steering medium like the other two because, on this definition it would tend to subsume them. In terms of the radical redefinition, money and power *are* technologies.[4]

Feenberg also seems to invoke the common sense definition when he writes of the 'elements' that comprise any given technology. At the bottom of any socio-historical manifestation of technology, he argues, there are 'neutral elements'. This sounds more like things, in the standard sense than people or situations. Feenberg is clear, though, that in themselves these elements are not technology, they merely represent potential until they are taken up, concatenated in socially determined designs and then used. But this leaves it unclear what it is about these things that makes them pre-technological, as distinct from pre-aesthetic, or pre-social objects. Conceiving people or situations in these 'pre' terms, as raw elements suggests a prevarication in the theory concerning the extent to which the essence of technology really is independent of any notion of a discrete class of pre-social, physical objects. There is, perhaps, a degree of slippage here between technology as thing or things and the idea of technology as attitudes embodied in a practice. This is problematic because without the distinction it is difficult to see how people might perceive neglected potentials in technology at any given time, yet this latter is necessary to the development of a design critique. If we are *in* our own society and this society codifies some objects as technical and that this is the only way that we can perceive them as such, then alternative potentials within the technology are going to be obscure to us. What Feenberg calls the 'capitalist technical code' selects which concatenations will become determinate and codifies them for us. We, recognising them as 'technology' then constitute them as such through our practice. If we want a design critique it will be necessary to find a way into this circle that gives us some leverage once we are there.

When addressing the problem of how we recognise the technological, Feenberg refers to a 'hermeneutics of technology'. This phrase is suggestive since it implies a number of possible ways into the circle just described. Feenberg is surely correct to maintain that defining technology is, first and foremost, an issue of interpretation. The point is not to postulate an extra or pre-social element in the definition of technology, but to insist that the theory includes in its account of the

---

[4] Feenberg tries to forestall this objection, urging his reader not to confuse technology with instrumentality, but here the point is different: if technology includes socially oriented strategies involving people and things then it is more likely than not to involve money and power as levers.

social constitution of technology some reference to the natural human animal and its inherent (ie. not coded by contemporary social forces) technical orientation. The essence of technology should not be conceived outside of social relations. The problem is that in theorising the technical encounter itself we need some notion of preparedness, of human beings as ready to hear that such and such is technology. Consistent with this, the circle can then broken into by the notion of a 'tradition' that is not reflected upon and which people acquire from their technology using forebears – Gadamer's position when dealing with similar issues of interpretation in the humanities (Gadamer 1975: 277-300). Something like this seems to be Feenberg's preferred route, as developed in his theory of 'Primary Instrumentalisation'.

Primary Instrumentalisation

To address the problem of what the defining essence of technology must be, Feenberg combines ontological and practical perspectives in his theory of instrumentalisation. Addressing the issue of the ontological status of the technological device, he argues that Heidegger was wrong to deny it the same 'world-disclosing' potential as other objects he (Heidegger) classifies as 'things'. In Heidegger's thought, things constitute the focus for 'gatherings', they are loci of meaning-significance. Things have 'intrinsic value and manifold connections with the human world and nature' (Feenberg 1999: 194). By focusing on them in the appropriate way we can discover the world as it is and find a kind of religious unity of ourselves and nature in and through this relationship. Technology, however, 'enframes' the world; it suppresses the connectedness of things and presents us instead with a direct route to our, instrumentally defined, goals. Feenberg argues that this is a humanistic prejudice on Heidegger's part. Devices can also open out onto an experience of world-disclosure. This insight is vital if we are to gain perspective on the role technology might play in more emancipated forms of social life. As Feenberg writes, even in the present the encounter with technology (for those who actually use it rather than its designers) '...constitutes an essential dimension of the contemporary struggle for a humane and liveable world' (1999: 199).

In his theory of primary instrumentalisation, Feenberg argues that two ontological moments precede and prefigure our understanding of an object as technological.[5] First, the thing is decontextualised – separated from its 'world' and exposed as 'containing technical schemas, potentials in human action systems' (1999: 203). Feenberg denies that he is developing a critique of science here, but the Marcusian regret attached to this process is unmistakeable in his observation that, 'Nature is fragmented into bits and pieces that appear as technically useful' (1999: 203). Decontextualisation is, though, the social inheritance, as it were, of a scientific perspective on objects – a way of focusing on their properties as discrete

---

[5] Feenberg refers to the moments in instrumentalisation as 'technical principles', but they are clearly centred on the life or genesis of objects – devices – illustrating the point made at the end of the previous section.

items. Yet Feenberg says that he intends no critique of science as such and is clearly aware of the dangers in politically motivated attacks on science.

The second ontological moment in the technical relation is the reduction of objects to their 'primary qualities'. In our encounter with the object it now appears bereft of distracting attachments and intrinsic meanings beyond the 'affordances' that it holds out for us. Technical objects enter our experience 'stripped of technically useless qualities' (1991: 203). There is slippage here, though. Recall that the object is not being altered in this process, it is entering social relations – it is the form of the technical encounter that we are supposed to be mapping. Nothing distinctive is introduced by this second moment, nothing that would distinguish the technical from any other kind of encounter. When I approach anything – a bit of paint on a palette, or a lathe – I necessarily look for affordances, else I will fail to adopt a practical orientation to the world and constantly run up against it instead.

Paradoxically, the first two moments of primary instrumentalisation seem to read too much and too little into the technical relation. Too much because Feenberg asks us to assume, with Heidegger, some kind of originary unity between the human being and the Being of the world. This unity is somehow broken up and we lose sight of it in technology's enframing of the world, although Feenberg does not see this as implicating technical devices in the same way that Heidegger does. But why should we believe in this founding unity? Why not postulate a fragmentary, disparate ontological order incompatible with this kind of first philosophy (Adorno 1966: 140)? Better than either of these routes would be to accept that as long as there have been people and a world there have been manifestations of the technical relation and that little perspective is to be gained on this by speculating about the stage that preceded it. The technical relation must be prefigured, to be sure, but we do not need an ontology of origins to understand how.

At the same time, Feenberg reads too little into the technical relation in that, by speculating in this way about the inherent ontological properties of things we actually lose our sense of the openness and indeterminacy of the technical that led us to seek a hermeneutics of technology. Feenberg objects to Heidegger that he views technology from a top-down perspective and so cannot conceive the device as leading us anywhere other than towards our instrumentally set goals. But, in a similar way, these ontological moments impose a kind of homogeneity onto the natural relations between humans and their environment – a kind of immanent choreography that cannot be justified rationally. These ideas are a theorisation of the grounding prejudice that prefigures our experience of the technical, but an alternative would be to embrace the indeterminacy discussed earlier and work out how it is that people always know and have always known what it was to be technical.

This alternative I call the *minimal technological attitude*. It starts with a hypothesis – that *x* is a technical object and not primarily an ergonomic, aesthetic or loving one. Just as with issues of meaning in the humanities, we initially have no way to be sure that this hypothesis is correct (Quine 1960: Davidson 1980). Its verification consists in unpacking connotations of the 'technical' in the course of further interactions with the problematic object. Thereby, a technical practice may be established. Just as radical interpretation of the speaker of an alien language involves experimenting with hypotheses about what they might mean – given that they, like us, are rational and operating in the same environment – so we must experiment with our attempts to make the technology work and this is done by forming hypotheses and trying them out. The advantage of the minimal technological attitude over the ontological moments in primary instrumentalisation is that it preserves the openness and indeterminacy of the technical relation and locates its conditions of possibility in the species character of the human being as a social animal. In what follows I hope to show that this pragmatic notion also meshes better with a realist stance on the technical object.

The second two moments in Feenberg's theory of Primary Instrumentalisation are practical and fill out admirably what assuming the minimal technological attitude might involve. The technical relation involves 'autonomisation'; an interruption in the way that feedback works between our acting upon something and its reaction. Normally, there is a principle of symmetry at work in our relations with things whereby if we hit them they redound back upon us, for instance. In the technical relation this principle is modified so that our energy is channelled away from us, perhaps amplified by being applied to the thing, which might be just the first object in a series. As Feenberg puts it, the Newtonian law of 'for every action an equivalent reaction' is circumvented as we become the initiator of action but sidestep its direct consequences, which are instead channelled through the technical system.

The final moment in primary instrumentalisation is 'positioning'. In order to exploit the inherent properties of objects, made peculiarly apparent, perhaps, as primary qualities, human beings must position themselves appropriately in order to autonomise. The technical relation involves us identifying the appropriate stance in order that we can bring 'to account' the benefits of autonomisation and act effectively upon the technical system (1999: 203). These two moments reflect the way in which tools are incorporated into basic structures of human action (Cf. Dewey 1997: 153-4). The process is mediated through the minimal technological attitude, in which we formulate and reformulate technical hypotheses. These latter involve different autonomisations and positionings – we experiment with ideas about how a device or system might work and how to position ourselves to make things happen with it. Our experimentation is guided by a *folk technology*, which tells us that, assuming the device or system is technological then there will be a position from which we can secure different degrees of autonomisation – in other words that the device or system exhibits some kind of relevant and discrete causal integration in its parts and that we can tighten, or render more precise, our causal descriptions of them.

Feenberg comments that the second two moments 'describe the form of action implied in Habermas's media theory' (1999: 203). He means by this that Habermas's systems sphere of society is that which is susceptible to description in terms that have people acting as if they were practically oriented towards technology.[6] Feenberg insists that 'The primary instrumentalisation lays out in

---

[6] On Habermas's use of action orientation concepts, see his (1991: 285-6). On the system sphere, see (1992: 235-282), and on integration (1991: 342).

skeletal fashion the basic technical orientation' (1999: 205). I think it is clear that its first two moments do more than this, however. To see this it is helpful to compare his critical theory with Habermas's much more conservative perspective. Both Habermas and Feenberg want to criticise technical systems only when they are used inappropriately. Both require critical standards that will disclose the limits of appropriate use. For Habermas this turns on the question of 'social integration': The steering of social behaviour is illegitimate if it is not grounded in evolutionary imperatives creating a generalised interest in not spending the time coordinating action through discourse. Illegitimate steering of social practices is regrettable because it means that areas of life are unnecessarily rendered routine and meaningless for their participants. This is what Feenberg means when he suggests that Habermas wants to get 'a whole social critique' out of that 'common core of attributes' possessed by all 'technical action systems and rationalities' (1999: 178).

Feenberg's alternative is to derive his critical standards from a logic that is immanent to the technological sphere properly understood. The technical relation as described in primary instrumentalisation is intended as a minimal specification of what technology is. Critique proper starts when we look at what it could be, freed from the fetter of capitalism. And yet, there is prevarication here as it seems that primary instrumentalisation involves a kind of violence, especially in its ontological dimensions, that Feenberg continues to find regrettable. Summarising his account of the skeletal basis of the technical, he writes that 'technology, in essence, decontextualises and manipulates its objects, it is non-reflective, indifferent to values, power-oriented, *and so on*. And that, no amount of change at the social level can alter' (1999: 216 my emphasis), hinting that there may be enough there upon which to base a social critique after all? Feenberg's position is complex because he wants to maintain that the technical sphere is necessarily and always underscored by attitudes that drew the fire of earlier generations of critical theorists – attitudes that are in some philosophically obscure sense, negative. At the same time, however, these attitudes only remain to the fore, dominant in our contemporary experience of technology, because of a peculiar affinity between primary instrumentalisation and capitalism – a particularly nasty social system for reasons that are, perhaps, not so obscure. From this standpoint Habermas is wrong to view strategic action or even the minimal technical relation as 'neutral' *and* mistaken in trying to base a critique of the overdevelopment of the system sphere on this neutral characterisation. For Feenberg, even the minimal specification does not disclose a level within the social constellation that defines the essence of technology that is untainted by morally regrettable connotations. Moreover, capitalism accentuates these and inhibits the natural tendency, which is also immanent to technology in its essence, to overcome them. Feenberg's is clearly the more radical view. In the remainder of this paper I want to try and preserve this radicalism while detaching it from its rather obscure ontological dimensions discussed in this section and integrating its insights into a more pragmatic frame of reference.

Technological Hegemony

One of Feenberg's most exciting theoretical insights and one which I try to exploit in the rest of this book, is the notion of a technological hegemony, which concerns the way that dominant social interests are reflected and reproduced in and through technology design. Technological hegemony centres on the real and perceived limits of the technical, which Feenberg sometimes refers to as 'the boundary of technique'. This has a dual character, which he describes as 'the ambivalence of technology'. It refers on one side to all the things that technology could really do for us at any given stage of development, given the appropriate employments (1991: 66). This is the *potential* of a technology to serve human interests. On the other side, technology is a limiting condition – a horizon on experimental ways of life that is imposed by material exigencies (1991: 59). Under this aspect, technology *limits* what we can hope to do and how we can hope to live. Technological hegemony is secured by controlling the dominant perception of what technology can do and of the limits it imposes; it is successful management of the ambivalence of technology.

It follows from what has been said above that these limits cannot be known: we always approach technology from within a society that pre-shapes our encounter with it, determining how it will appear to us and what we will try to do with it. The appearance of technology is partly determined by design. Feenberg compares technology design to law, in that it tends to circumscribe a field of action and behaviour as appropriate and correct, while including built-in prohibitions on deviant actions (cf Woolgar in Law 1991). What we will do with a technology, however, goes on within limits that are set by our 'margin for maneouvre', which varies with our social status. Design is an important factor in controlling this margin and is, therefore, the site of a conflict within which hegemony may be won and lost. This is the significance of those periods at the birth of a new technology, when no one is really sure what it is and what it might be used for (Feenberg 1999: 96-7; see also Bijker and Hughes 1989).

Although design is, in this sense, political, the conflicts and decisions that are played out here are not driven by conventional political ideology but by the codification of interests as technical requirements. They are built into our ways of seeing the potential of a technology – what it is for and how it should be used. Feenberg argues, against David Noble (1984), that it is not because managers are ideologically predisposed to choose nasty technology that we get production lines and other inhuman, routinising and de-skilling uses of technology. It is because those designs are the ones that represent *technically* superior options. This perception is formed in what Feenberg theorises as the 'condensation' of social and technical requirements in design standards that are hegemonic. Under capitalism, this condensation takes the form of a technological rationality which itself becomes the dominant form of reason; it comes to 'appear more and more as the very definition of rationality' (1991: 70). This 'technological rationality', 'dominant technological rationality', or 'authoritarian technological rationality' Feenberg defines as neither ideology (it is not the presence of false beliefs about society within the design process), nor a neutral requirement of technique (it is not instrumental reason as such). Rather, it 'stands at their intersection' (1991: 14) and is overdetermined by the power differential that runs through capitalist societies (1991: 69). This power differential, which initially traces to the division of labour (1991: 15) and then traverses other 'terrains of struggle privileged by post-Marxism' (1991: 16), is itself an effect of the technical sphere. In other words, it only emerges once technological rationality has become hegemonic. Technological rationality is the form of hegemony in technical politics that is specific to capitalism. It condenses technical and social imperatives in designs that actualise the potential of technical know-how at any given time, in ways that serve the dominant social interests. Under capitalism, the raw elements and principles of primary instrumentalisation are found to be in tune with a social system that is largely based on domination. Hence, hegemonic technological rationality can be depicted as the apex of a triangle of forces, with technical reason at one corner and social power differentials at the other. This is represented graphically in figure 1.1.

Each point in the triangle works to reinforce the others. Technological rationality, technical reason and the power differential constitute a single, integrated system. The sides of the triangle are axes of legitimacy, along which each point reinforces the other by making the domination of current technical norms appear natural and obvious.

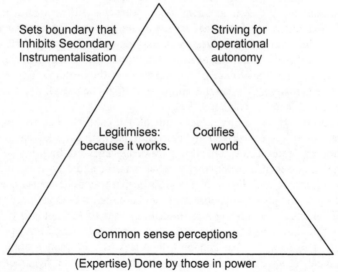

Technological Rationality

Sets boundary that
Inhibits Secondary
Instrumentalisation

Striving for
operational
autonomy

Legitimises:
because it works.

Codifies
world

Common sense perceptions

(Expertise) Done by those in power

Technical Reason/   **Power Differential**
Instrumentalism   **in Society**

Figure 1.1: Hegemonic Technological Rationality

The Power Differential

The power differential arises when the technical attitude, or the third and fourth moments in primary instrumentalisation, is applied to human and social objects. Initially, this is the function of capitalist managers but it gradually extends to involve administrators and bureaucrats in the highly regulated social formation that is modern capitalism. The power differential is maintained when these groups seek to maximise their own and their organisations' 'operational autonomy'. Strategies to achieve this are justified as 'rational' and therefore irresistible, with reference to the codification of the world by technological rationality – this is represented by the right side of the triangle, reading down from technological rationality to the power differential. At the same time, this struggle for operational autonomy reinforces the hegemonic power, since it is consistent with the capitalist codification of things as economic resources and of actors as fundamentally competitive (represented by reading up from the power differential to technological rationality).

Hegemonic technological rationality works through and is embodied in codifications of real objects and situations that are co-extensive with, or perhaps isomorphic with, the instrumental criterion found in technical reasoning proper. Feenberg writes that we readily accept the application of technical reason to human states of affairs because our deepest categorical experiences (1991: 123) under capitalism are reproduced in it – we expect the world to involve detachment and action from above to exert control and so are unsurprised to find it in social experience. At the same time, since this is indeed the way that those with power operate, when we come to exercise the power differential ourselves this will be our own procedure, regardless of political ideology. This axis of mutually legitimating forces is represented in figure 1.1 by the base of the triangle.

The social influence on design is not, then, a set of substantive ideologically driven requirements of the capitalist class. Rather, it is mediated through the perceived need, under capitalist conditions, for those in power (controlling organisations etc.) to select strategies that maximise their operational autonomy. Taken together, the resulting web of strategies is embedded in capitalist rule – its systematic domination (1991: 79). The model of organisation that prioritises operational autonomy itself derives from a strategic-instrumental conception of the world that presupposes technological rationality. Feenberg writes that '...to exist...' in capitalist conditions, '...organisations must 'encode' their technical environment,' and that, '...the technical code... is the principle of organisational identity and survival' (1991: 80). Codification of the technical environment is the condition of existence for those with power *and* their primary activity. It is how they go about interpreting themselves and their sphere of operations. They justify their choice of strategies with reference to the technical code, which is '...most essentially the rule under which technical choices are made in view of preserving operational autonomy' (1991: 80). The hegemony of the technical code means that those choices are overdetermined to seem obvious, technical in character rather than ethical or political. As Feenberg puts it, '...social and political leadership falls to those performing a specific *technical* function, the management of labor,'

(1991: 59) for whom, 'the assembly line ...appears as technical progress because it extends the kind of administrative rationality on which capitalism already depends' (1991: 82).

Technical Reason

Under the hegemony of technological rationality, the decontextualising and manipulative dimensions of primary instrumentalisation form the basis for the technical practice of managers and elite groups whose main responsibility is to maximise their own freedom by manipulating subject populations. This is represented in the diagram by reading from right to left (from the power differential to technical reason) along the base of the triangle. At the same time, those in power are associated with the knowledge content denoted by the technical sphere and in this way the technical itself enjoys continuous social validity and esteem, mediated through the category of the expert – the significance of reading the same line from left to right. The system rests on the continued success of technical practice in generating solutions to practical problems, including problems generated by the system itself, such as environmental damage.

The left hand side of the triangle, going up from technical reason to technological rationality, highlights the legitimating function of the on-going popular belief in technology for the hegemonic rationality. Technological rationality is closely linked to technical (instrumental) reasoning and indeed both are tainted forms, unpleasant ways of approaching the world in Feenberg's moralised ontology. They differ, however, at least potentially, as far as the ends or boundaries of reason are concerned. As seen above, on Feenberg's account technical reason emerges from primary instrumentalisation – it is the third and fourth moments sedimented into a mind-set. It forms the worldview of technicians and other elite groups. Feenberg rarely clarifies what he means by 'rationality' or competing 'rationalities'. However, it seems inescapable that users and especially designers of technology must engage in what critical theory traditionally referred to as 'instrumental' or 'means-end' reasoning in relation to the objects they work with. This is not mentioned explicitly in the account of primary instrumentalisation,[7] but Feenberg appears to acknowledge that such reasoning must always be present wherever there is technology when he writes,

> Means-end rationality is no doubt an unsurpassable dimension of modern industrialism, but it will have quite different consequences in cultures that measure success differently, define the legitimate domain of optimisation differently and have different ends in view. (1991: 126)

---

[7] Indeed, part of the point of Feenberg's instrumentalisation theory is, perhaps, to go beyond the generalisations of Marcuse (1964) and others about the pernicious consequences of 'formal' reason and to trace its history, precisely to reach a more nuanced understanding of the kind of thinking that is intrinsic to technical activity and to separate this from the social consequences with which it has been associated since Weber. See Feenberg's comments on Marcuse in his (1999: 162).

His observation here – that instrumental reason, or rather the sub-part of it here called 'means-end rationality', is consistent with any number of social outcomes – is entirely valid and an important corrective to thinkers within the critical theory tradition who see some kind of inherent menace in all instrumental reasoning. However, there is a distinction to be drawn as far as 'ends' are concerned between those of the individual technologist working on a project and those of society as a whole. The former are always instrumental goals of the technologists' action, while the latter involves situating these goals socially, with reference to ethics and other value systems. According to Feenberg, this ambivalence at the neutral heart of technology is a function of which 'aspect' we prioritise. Basic techniques are neutral in the sense that they are open to different social encodings, but not with respect to the ends they prescribe for the specific objects they conceive as means. The latter is a 'founding bias' (1991: 170) associated with all primary instrumentalisation, but it need not prevent the resultant technique, or technology from playing a role in a different socially prescribed set of ends, broadly conceived.

In any society, I would argue, the technical in general will mark off an orientation to the world that is, in its innermost core, instrumental in the narrow sense that it will seek to isolate and use bits of nature as means to achieve some ends. But the ends in question, for the technical *as a whole* can be varied, according to the kind of civilization we live in. In capitalism, under hegemonic technological rationality, the boundaries are set very narrow, by the requirement that technology be consistent with maintaining the power differential. But this need not always be the case. The ends of a specific technical endeavour will always be tightly prescribed from the point of view of the technologist working on that project. In order to be used at all, however, these same ends must be redescribed in terms set by a broader perspective that situates them in context. Only in the capitalist context, for example, have aesthetic criteria tended to disappear from the social descriptions of technology. Contextual description of the ends of tool use has been de-ritualised and reduced to its functional aspect, reflecting condensation in design of the capitalist drive for control.

The problem with Feenberg's, highly sophisticated, model of the hegemony of technological rationality is that the instrumentalism at its core is too readily associated with empowered social positions. Repeatedly, Feenberg emphasises that technologists, managers, those in control of production and related social processes come at their objects, be they things, people, processes 'from above'. They seek to manipulate and control them in order to achieve the ends of maximal operational autonomy. In short, these subject positions (manager, owner, technician) are held to be socially empowered because they are subjects of the technical relation, while those who are disempowered (workers, excluded minorities, the environment) are so because they are its objects. As such, Feenberg argues, they necessarily perceive and experience the basic, technical relation differently. Setting aside the question mark raised over this equivalence (technically knowledgeable = socially empowered) by instances of technically knowledgeable disempowered people, like computer hackers, and their converse the (all-too-common) technologically challenged manager, the real problem here is an epistemological conundrum familiar to environmentalists.[8]

Those who exercise power through effective use of technology have access to the real technological thing. They can see it and possess an understanding of what it can do; they are less limited to interfacing with it in a prescribed fashion than those who are simply presented with the finished artefact and told to work. As objects, the latter group cannot access the inner reality of the artefact and so their attempts to interfere directly in its workings and to make suggestions about its immediate sphere of operations are likely to be interpreted as perverse, wrongly motivated, perhaps even self-destructive. Technocracy, or the rule of technological rationality is, in this practical sense, a circular or self-referential system. Feenberg needs an opposed pole within the system, a place from which to start if we are to gain any sense of a real social alternative that we can grasp from our vantage point in the present. Feenberg acknowledges that this was the problem left unresolved by his critical theory forebears, who mounted a critique of instrumentalism that was so thorough-going they left themselves marooned with no, non-instrumentalised social reference points in which they could ground their critique. His theory of technological hegemony is intended to overcome this, by clarifying what he calls the margin of manoeuvre of the oppressed. Two possibilities offer themselves in this context. The notion of a progressive politics within the field of design itself and a theory of the reality of technology from which to derive clarity as to what the boundary of technique might consist in.

According to Feenberg, counter-hegemonic forces probe the technical boundary – the limits on what technology can do *and* the veracity of hegemonic assertions that it must do *x* or *y*. The problem is, though, that on his conception of primary instrumentalisation it affords no space for such contestation. Here, I submit, his vision has been affected by that instinctive aversion to instrumentalism that runs so strongly through the critical theory tradition since the Frankfurt School. The problem traces to the fact that Feenberg has been insufficiently thorough-going in his effort to detach technical reason from its implication in social domination. There is a sense in which technical control is *personally empowering* for individuals in a way that is not only not regrettable but essential to our personal growth and to the development of a better society. Feenberg himself argues that breast feeding is a 'success oriented' technique, corresponding to primary instrumentalisation (1999: 173) and it is difficult to reconcile this with his insistence that 'capitalism has a unique relation to this aspect of technique' (1991: 182) or his agreement with Marcuse that there is 'pre-established harmony between the fragmenting, decontextualizing dimension of technical rationality and capitalism' (1991: 176). Moreover, unless critics of technology are themselves a bit strategic in their own activities – including viewing others as means and

---

[8] The epistemological problem can be presented in the form of two questions:
  1. Who is to contest design, if not people already mired in the technocracy?
  2. How does anyone in the present gain any sense of what the boundaries of contemporary technique are, really?

opportunities – it is difficult to see that they have a margin of manoeuvre within technocratic constraints.

Feenberg might object to this that his counter-hegemonic questioning is rooted less in experimental, oppositional sub-cultures of personal empowerment through dabbling, than in immanent potentialities of technology itself. While the former may offer limited experiences of personal empowerment, they do not touch upon the broader social reality of technology use. Primary instrumentalisation and the instrumental attitude that go along with it reflect the technical relation in a corrupted and stymied condition, rather than affording any privileged epistemological perspective on the technological proper – its essential properties. We require standards for the appropriate social ends of technology rather than a practical epistemology and Feenberg provides them in his theory of secondary instrumentalisation.

Secondary Instrumentalisation

For Feenberg, probing the limits of the technical consists less in hands-on tinkering with technology than in a technological sub-politics that tries to act upon the horizons of technological development.[9] The aim of such a shift is to alter the core logic of technical design processes themselves. As we have seen, technical reason incorporates a kind of inherent congruence with hierarchical, administered society. Viewing an object or situation in this way involves us in all of the moments of primary instrumentalisation: We are detached, come at the object from above, ask what it can do for us and not where it is in the world, and we try to exploit it by making it work for us. This is why primary instrumentalisation 'offers no foothold for a socialist alternative' (1991: 188-9). For Feenberg, shifting the horizon on technical development involves inculcating a greater awareness within design communities that they are a part of the systems that they produce. Feenberg invokes here a 'self-referential logic of action... that would have as its goal not escape from the community to a commanding position above it, but internal self-development in common with others' (1991: 113). Designers must have their perspective altered to accommodate the values and interests of society and in this way their practice will be opened up to both perspectives described in the double aspect theory above. The success and desirability of a technology design would be measured not merely in terms of the efficiency and productivity gains associated with it, as at present, but with reference to criteria that affect all of our interests – including interests in the well-being of others and of the natural environment. Feenberg gives the example of air quality, which ought to be included as a factor in the design of technical systems like transportation (1991: 113) (although we

---

[9] This way of construing technical politics aligns it with Ulrich Beck's (1992) sub-politics, which is focused on issues of risk and the effective management of environmental threats posed by technology to subject populations. See Feenberg (1999: 120) and chapter 6 below.

may add that once it was, it would have to be decomposed into a series of targets for discrete sub-systems, that is, translated into the language of technologists).

Capitalism, though, actually stymies the development of technology and of *technical reason itself* in such a direction. The second part of this is perhaps the more surprising, since primary instrumentalisation was supposed to have laid bare the neutral skeletal form of technical reason. Feenberg is quite explicit:

> ...the technical enterprise itself is immanently disposed to address the demands we formulate as potentialities, but... it is artificially truncated in modern industrial societies. Opening technical development to the influence of a wider range of values is a technical project requiring broad democratic participation. Radical democratisation can thus be rooted in the very nature of technology... (1991: 19)

The forces that oppose the capitalist codification of technology, then, are immanent to the technical sphere itself. According to Feenberg, 'the essence of technology ...includes a secondary level that works with dimensions of reality from which the primary instrumentalisation abstracts' (1999: 205). Capitalism is now accused not of an affinity with the violence of primary instrumentalisation (although it is guilty of that too) but of introducing a corruption into the design of technology itself so that the primary level dominates our experience. Any society would have to work out the relationships between primary and secondary instrumentalisation (in this sense they are analytical categories, like Habermas's system and lifeworld) but only capitalism obliges us to experience primary instrumentalisation in the way that we do. This is why there is no possibility of experiencing a manifestation of technology that is neutral. Capitalism 'reifies' (1991: 188) the primary instrumentalisation as 'neutral' technology in action, but this is a false representation. In any social system, the experience of technology also contains a secondary instrumentalisation, whereby '...technique must be integrated with the natural, technical and social environments to support its functioning' (1999: 205). Feenberg calls this secondary instrumentalisation 'realization' or 'concretisation' (1999: 205) and in it some of the violence with which the technical relation was established is compensated for.[10]

Like its primary form, secondary instrumentalisation has four forms. Each corresponds to a moment in primary instrumentalisation and, perhaps, represents the route to a kind of natural remedy for the violence done by the technologising attitude in its first phase. The first moment of secondary instrumentalisation is 'concretisation' (1991: 189). What Feenberg has in mind here is a process whereby technology is 'recontextualised' in a way that involves the resurfacing of interests and connections that were suppressed in the primary phase, such as environmental protection modifications. This has less to do with restoring the object of the technical relation to its rightful place in the natural world than its successful integration into larger, networked systems involving other contemporary

---

[10] Feenberg argues that technology has 'integrative potentialities' that enable it to 'repair the damage it does' (1991: 182).

technology (1999: 205). The point is that the brute separateness that gets imposed on things in primary instrumentalisation is overcome by a sense of their being part of a stable lifeworld or meaningful environment, which is the context for its subsequent use. This is related to the second moment, which Feenberg calls 'aestheticisation'. As already emphasised above, it is only in capitalism that tools are de-aestheticised and deprived of their meaning-significance in social life. In secondary instrumentalisation these and other values are condensed, alongside the technical and social values necessary to capitalist domination, in final designs. Even under capitalism, though, there is some aesthetic investment in the object, which enables people to relate to it as an acceptable element in experience. I will return to this theme in chapter three.

The third and fourth moments in secondary instrumentalisation are 'vocation' and 'collegiality' respectively. It is a defining feature of technology that, when used, it amplifies and channels the intended action of its human user, rather than simply thwarting them with the normal dullness of the inert, or through a proportionate negative, or adverse response. In secondary instrumentalisation, technology recovers some of its power to impact upon the person who uses it. In vocation the reciprocity between human action and the reaction of the thing that was suppressed in primary instrumentalisation is now 'recovered at a higher level' (1991: 189). This higher level is not physical but concerns an investment of identity in the human actor, associated with the decontextualised object. Hence, the person who works with wood finds that this reacts back upon them, transforming them into a carpenter. In modern societies this can take the form of professionalisation (1999: 206) and, as we will see in chapter four, the idea offers insights into the strangeness of the computer hacker, who cannot find a niche within existing professional structures. In the idea of collegiality, Feenberg suggests that every hegemonic codification encounters a tactical resistance in the secondary phase of instrumentalisation. In collegiality, workers and others appropriate their tools by finding alternative ways of coming at them, rather than simply assuming the 'position' assigned to them by the design of the technology. Disaffected workers who played 'Doom' on the company intranet would, perhaps, illustrate this principle.

My critique of secondary instrumentalisation depends upon denying the practical utility of the first two moments, while incorporating the insights of the third and fourth into a more pragmatic critical framework. The notion of a more integrated and mediated use of technology is appealing because it suggests a friction-less accommodation of new technical ideas by society. Changes to the work process become smoother and facilitate more communication. However, as we will see when we look more closely at how PCs have been assimilated into capitalist society, the idea of secondary instrumentalisation does not give us standards with which to assess the desirability of a new horizon on technology development and technical integration. Similarly, just because a work station is aesthetically pleasing does not entail that it is a zone of liberation. What concretisation and re-aestheticisation seem to suggest is that there is an appropriate aesthetic critique of technology that is necessarily consonant with socialist values and this seems to be what Feenberg has in mind. Writing of the superior, more integrated technology that would be possible in a free society, he argues that this will be defined with reference to human well being:

> The values in terms of which this well-being is defined, such as beauty, health, free expression and growth, may not have a scientific status and may not be the object of universal agreement, but neither are they merely personal preferences as modern value nihilism would have it. They arise in our lived experience of nature and have a history in which they have been the object of rational reflection and criticism. (1999: 165)

There is a very important point being made here about the place of aesthetic principles in social critique. Habermas has been justly criticised for leaving aesthetics out of his sociological theory (Duvenage 2003), for example, whereas earlier versions of critical theory were directly associated with specific movements within art and culture. I will return to this issue in chapter three and suggest that while Feenberg is correct to recommend standards of this type, his position would be greatly strengthened were he to draw less on the naturalist modernism of Frank Lloyd Wright and more on the aggressive, political modernism associated with Brecht's realism.

The third and fourth moments of secondary instrumentalisation say nothing of the technical artefact itself and are addressed instead to the forms of subjectivity associated with it. As such, they define the field of technical politics proper, understood in terms of human orientations towards the technical in principle and towards specific technological artefacts. We need to know, however, if they solve the epistemological problem opened up at the end of the last section. What is it that technical people, as subjects of the technical relation, see that we, as its objects, do not? And how does their perspective relate to the issues of social power involved in technological hegemony? I will deal with these questions in turn.

Primarily, real physical objects form the locus of technical activity. The positioning and autonomisation that Feenberg describes are orientations, in Habermas's sense, that we can assume towards the world. They arise most naturally not in our relation to other people but in relation to physical things. It is natural – or perhaps 'quasi-natural' – to come at a stick and see if it might be used as a bat, or to get fruit from high branches of a tree. It is less natural that we should approach another individual, or a social situation with similar ideas in mind. There, the normal thing would be to communicate, to recognise the other as like one's self in various respects, and so on. The splitting off of some human relationships as subject to the 'technical relation' is an evolutionary accomplishment – for the child who has learned to engineer friendships in playground politics and for the society that has become too complex to organise all of its functions through rational deliberation and debate. For earlier critical theorists, these did not seem like achievements so much as moments in the loss of a superior, more peaceful form of co-existence. Feenberg accepts that the minimal technical relation is natural, but insists that it is corrupted under capitalism so that people cannot see it for what it is. The corruption involves an extension of its authority, so to speak, which is the target of Habermas's critical theory. For Feenberg this is insufficient: the technical relation that is over-extended in capitalism is a perversion of the technical relation that would open up the full potential within technology *and* it is over-extended relative to the scope of even a healthy, non-perverted version.

The problem for Feenberg's view is that unless we separate out some minimal specification of the real technological object – alongside the minimal technological attitude and folk technology – then we will have no critical standard against which to assess the boundaries that arise when we probe technology's ambivalent limits. There must be a real technological object – something that corresponds to our folk technological expectations – just as there must be a real environment around rational interlocutors at the scene of radical interpretation (Davidson 1980). The questions are, who knows what that object is? What can it do? Who can we trust to tell us? Feenberg argues that technologists and technology users have very different perspectives on the technical object. Technology experts confront its users. Technologists' perspective on technical objects is that of knowledge, while, as expert, they hold the social position of power. Similarly, technology users are ignorant of the factors behind design and this is the mark of their disempowerment. In the first perspective it is possible to see the technical elements, discussed earlier, that must be concatenated to produce specific technologies. Any number of concatenations are possible, on the basis of the neutral, technical elements available to any given society. As Feenberg writes, this is where the social determination comes in:

> ...it is not merely because a technology works that it is chosen for development over many other equally coherent configurations of technical elements. Were that the case, then by analogy one could also explain the choice of individual sentences in speech by their grammatical coherence. (1991: 82)

The analogy with language is highly suggestive. What is needed, to ground a counter-hegemonic practice is something corresponding to the 'truth-conditionality' that makes some utterances relevant, useful, truly meaningful, rather than simply 'well-formed'. In other words, just as it is true that all instantiated technologies bear the impress of a mesh of social determinations, so they must also respect the real physical limitations set, internally, by technology at that time.

Feenberg could not accept this because it affords an epistemological priority to the perspective of technical experts. The force of this objection, however, is mitigated by two considerations. First, the technologists in question do not here include those who operate social management systems. Those kinds of expert trade on association with people who have real technical expertise only under the current hegemony. If we accept the constellar definition of technology as the application of the minimal technological attitude to the manipulation of real objects, then we can break that connection. In short, Feenberg is too quick to postulate an equivalence between perspective on the technological object and social subject position – a function of his too ready conflation of the technical relation with real objects and social techniques of domination. If we refuse this move then we can accept that technical expertise is epistemically significant and that technology design must involve social processes beneath the institutional level denoted by terms like 'user' and 'expert'. This position may be less than ideal relative to the traditional left wing goal of equality. However, it is warranted by the facts of the case and rendered more politically acceptable, even necessary, by changes in the relationship between expert knowledge and social status caused by the diffusion of personal computing. As society computerises it is a necessary part of what has become known as reflexive modernisation that we all acquire greater knowledge about these machines.[11]

Although it is true that a realist perspective on technology grants experts a socially determinate epistemological priority, this is less significant now than it has been in the past. With the spread of personal computers we are more likely to see the appearance of technologically defined sub-groups who break with the technocracy and possess the knowledge to explore the boundaries of potentiality associated with the technology. Increasingly, the acquisition of technical knowledge in de-formalised settings takes on a social and political significance, defining technical politics.

Technical Politics and the Personal Computer

In the chapters that follow I will suggest that revising Feenberg's framework in light of the criticisms developed here enables the development of a more critical perspective on the personal computer than we find in Feenberg's own reflections on the technology to date. Writing about the PC, Feenberg notes that computer technology was marketed in this form before anyone really knew what it was for. Subsequently, the PC was codified by technological rationality, primarily into an instrument of social control. This codification was mediated by engineer-experts. Rather than exploit the communicative potential of the PC, which was well-known in the scientific and technical communities from very early on (Hafner and Lyon 1996), they preferred to design machines that enhanced management control over the labour process. As Feenberg points out, this design orientation – evident perhaps in the early, mainframe based Management Information Systems and in command-line interfaces of the mid to late 1980s – exemplifies his observations on the condensation of social and technical imperatives in the capitalist technical code:

---

[11] 'Reflexive modernisation' is the idea that as well as originating a constant flow of social and cultural changes, modernity necessitates a constant reflection on itself as the source of those changes. Hence, as we get more science and technology, so we have a discourse on the risks associated with having more science and technology. This discourse then affects the kind of science and technology we get, along with all the other determining factors. I am suggesting that as computer technology increasingly supports innovations with broad social and cultural significance, so an increasing part of this reflexive discourse consists in autonomous computing as a cultural practice. I will explain this idea further below.

The place computers are intended to hold in social life is intimately connected with their design. Systems designed for hierarchical control are congruent with rationalistic assumptions that treat the computer as an automaton intended to command or replace workers in decision-making roles. Democratically designed systems must instead respond to the communicative dimension of the computer through which it facilitates the self-organisation of human communities, including those technical communities the control of which founds modern hegemonies. (1991: 108)

It is not because engineers believed in overt capitalist ideology that they tended to prefer inaccessible systems that supported centralised and hierarchical organisational models. Rather, this preference was consistent with 'rationalistic assumptions' (technical reason) and with the desire to maintain their own operational autonomy in relation to the machine. Feenberg points out that the top-down uses of computers at this time neglected to exploit innovations within computer science that held out alternative potentials, including the enhancement of communication as an integrating factor in social life.

He refers in particular to the development of Artificial Intelligence. In the work of computer scientists Terry Winograd and Fernando Flores (1986), the theoretical foundations were established for machines that could interact with people in sophisticated and yet accessible ways. They could furnish users with environments that responded to their needs and did not require them to rely on a technician, or to master an arcane computer language to achieve their goals. At the same time that this work was being done, in the mid-1980s, the graphical user interface began to transform the way that the computer was presented to people. This involved a metaphoric environment at the screen designed both to shield the user from machine complexity and to facilitate more autonomy for him/her than was possible using top-down systems, which normally just cycled through a limited number of screens feeding prompts to the user related to the performance of each new task. The design of these interfaces was collaborative rather than hierarchical. Participatory design ensured that users 'walked through' programs before they were marketed, testing them for ease of use and reliability. The new environments were not linear but open for people to navigate, taking the machine through multifarious state shifts just by pointing and clicking with a mouse. It was these 'user friendly interfaces' that spearheaded the rapid diffusion of personal computers in the 1990s. They represented a major departure from 'technical reason' towards a more integrated, human environment for workers. In this way, they met Feenberg's criteria for more aesthetic designs, as well as breaking the hold of engineers, with their rationalistic assumptions, on the design process.

However, capitalism has adapted to the social diffusion of the new interfaces. Much has been written about the levelling down of organisations, the 'flattening' of hierarchies and so on, but the fundamental logic of the system, like the basic lines of social cleavage referred to above, remain unaffected. If anything, the new interfaces have actually closed off many of the expressive and communicative possibilities that computers seemed to present themselves in the 1980s and early 1990s. This suggests that Feenberg's critique has not hit the mark with regard to the implication of technology in capitalist social processes. It is becoming increasingly clear, for instance, that the notion of a friendly, easy to use even playful technology is itself ideologically suspect. The contemporary interface has the function of denying the user access to the underlying mechanics of the PC and so is actually constraining. At the same time it is a source of distractions and 'entertainment' – ideology in the crudest sense. This observation is related to the point made in the previous section concerning the necessity for realism in technology studies. Feenberg writes:

> Engineers typically assume (as does modern common sense) that the technical device is actually identical with what they make of it and relates only externally to the society in which it is found; in fact it is a rich manifold that incorporates engineering parameters along with many others. ...the self-same device is subject to description in many discourses... none of which is 'fundamental'. (1999: 215-6)

It is true that the modern PC is a complex, multi-layered machine and that we relate to all of those levels through different metaphoric devices and constructions (Coyne 1995). However, while the reality of the machine level, so to speak, never surfaces, it remains the case that some levels of description are more profound than others, in the simple sense that the second class of descriptions presuppose and supervene upon the first. For every metaphor applied to account for the behaviour of an object on the screen there must be a corresponding set of bits flipped, zeroes and ones, lines of code compiled and so on. It may not be the case that there is one foundational level, but it is true that the physical underscores them all and that engineering and programming discourses are privileged in the pragmatic sense that they work closer to this level of description.[12] The interface obscures the real computer and this matters; it has practical consequences.

In particular, if we are to apply the critical standards in Feenberg's theory we need to know how open our computer mediated communication is. How subject is it to unseen regulation and surveillance? To what extent is the information we receive from search engines and other networked sources filtered? Who sets the filters on our browsers and how is their performance measured? To answer these questions requires technical knowledge. The importance of this knowledge – the significance to assign each of its points, if you like, is relative to our goals at any given stage. I am not interested in what line of C++ determined that my avatar's head fell off to the left rather than to the right, but I have a very real concern to know if my boss knows I am playing this game on the company machine. If I can stop her knowing then that will be extremely useful too. The theoretical point is that without a heightened reflexive knowledge that works on the technical level we will be unable to make critical assessments of the relative value of a system as facilitating communication and education. We need to know what the system is doing *really* and what it is capable of doing if we are going to develop a critique.

---

[12] Our folk technology tells us that the impression of having 'deleted' a file using the right click mouse method is less reliable, or 'true', than when we use the fatal 'rm *'.

Probing the boundaries of the technical presupposes the availability of technical understanding and so this availability needs to become a criterion, alongside the others developed by Feenberg (principally communication and education) for the progressive character of a design. Within contemporary computer culture there are two sub-cultural groups that are clearly involved in precisely this kind of activity – hackers and game modders – and, as subsequent chapters will show, both are having effects on interface design.

Feenberg's aesthetic criteria can also be criticised in this perspective. As seen in the previous section, he espouses naturalism for technology design based on the idea that well-being and a more integrated, holistic experience of the world may be facilitated by this. The critique just advanced of the naturalistic user interface subverts this, however, in the same way that Modernist critiques of naturalism in literature worked to subvert the ideal of a 'natural' order reflected in and reinforced by artistic representations. In fact, people often have to be forced to face up to reality in a process that can involve strategies of shock and various kinds of alienation effect designed to draw attention to the medium itself. Only in this way can we get people to look past the representation to reassess the real for themselves and renegotiate their relationship with it. Feenberg is certainly right to argue for an aestheticised relationship with technology, but he wrongly counterposes the natural and aesthetic to the technical. Technology is, as I have tried to argue throughout the current chapter, a natural part of the human condition and a natural orientation of the human animal. As such, it is inherently aesthetic too. The mechanical, austere and challenging interfaces on older operating systems were, in a sense, consistent with a more realist aesthetic of technology design.

Feenberg's work provides the conceptual resources with which to radicalise contemporary critical theory. It tells of the importance of applying aesthetic criteria to our way of life in all of its dimensions, including the technical. Contemporary critical theory, especially Habermas's work, remains too narrowly focused on the issue of social integration and so misses a host of ways in which contemporary technology design encroaches upon the texture of social life with objectionable consequences. Feenberg broadens the focus of critique so that we are no longer concerned only with whether technology is an appropriate means for co-ordinating action and can return to critical theory's traditional preoccupation with its role in broader processes of social domination. In this context Feenberg's insight that capitalism actually stymies technological development – especially in relation to technology as a vocation and as a locus of individual and collective initiative and experimentation – becomes particularly important. In the next chapter I turn to the historical origins of the personal computer. Conflicting social interests and ideological perspectives motivated different versions of the PC idea. Subjecting these to closer scrutiny discloses a more nuanced struggle than the one described in the 'engineers versus the people' mythology.

Chapter 2

Hacking the First Personal Computers

Introduction

The history of the personal computer is in many ways a perfect illustration of Feenberg's theoretical account of the social construction of technology. Many of the 'elements' that make up the personal computer such as using binary code as the basis for interacting with physical data storage systems; using electric pulses to represent data; the principle of using a processor to apply instructions to data; storing programs in a medium independent of the machine (the hardware/software distinction), for example, were all in existence by the 1950s. In that decade a number of small computers were even marketed, aimed at commercial clients (Ceruzzi 2000: 41). In the second half of the 1950s random access memory discs were invented by IBM and by the early 1960s transistors – integrated circuits – had begun to displace vacuum tubes as the basis for physical memory in most of the large computer systems around the world. Some computers used screens to display information to their human operatives. These developments all seem to anticipate the decision to concentrate the operations of a computer within the physical sphere of operations of the human individual. It is important to notice that they do not do so. Each one of these innovations has a history of its own, independent of that of the personal computer. Human agents, operating under specific social conditions, determined through their actions that the available technical elements would be concatenated together in each particular way.

Most of the early experimentation with computers was carried out by the military. As is well known, British efforts to crack German codes during World War II provided an important impetus to the drive to automate complex calculations, for example. Prior to the mid-1960s, computers were large unwieldy things that most people never saw, found only in elite research institutions. The computers were guarded and access to them was provided only via gatekeeper-technicians. Even mathematicians and other academics who wanted to use the computer had to submit their programs to the technicians and then wait to get the results back. Commercial systems were dedicated to organisation-specific functions. For computing power to become socially diffuse and accessible to all it had first to be dislodged from the grip of these powerful social forces. For that to happen, someone had to be sufficiently fascinated by the idea of the computer to want to try. More accurately, disparate groups of people with diverse motivations sought to appropriate the computer and in so doing they produced the idea and practice of 'personal computing'. In this way the technical elements that form the material basis of computing as we know it entered the constellation of social forces that constituted it as the technology we now recognise as the PC.

The 1960s witnessed the emergence of computer hacking. 'Hacking' at this time denoted intense engagement with a technical system, usually with the aim of getting the system to do something other than the function intended for it by its designer. The first hackers were graduate students and social misfits who gained access to computers at the Massachusetts Institute of Technology, primarily by moving into the rooms that held them at night, when the machines were left on and the 'official' technicians were at home. This group established behaviours and an ethos that has been associated with computer hackers ever since. Among their number was the inventor of the first computer game, *Space War*. A second group of hackers emerged in a more diffuse way all over the US in the second half of the 1970s. These people were also passionately engaged with computers and they began the process of moulding the disparate elements that make up the PC. They were the people who were truly responsible for personal computing, since they only gained access to computers by building their own, in garages and bedrooms, often from DIY kits. Of decisive significance in this history was the marketing of the first PC, the Altair 8800, which was sold as a kit through an advertisement in the magazine 'Popular Electronics' in 1975.

In its inception and early phases, the PC represented computer technology codified not by capital and dominant social groups, but shaped by a distinctive sub-culture. The PC idea and the early practice of personal computing provide insight into the processes whereby social forces actively contest what a technology is for, how it should be used and what it should look and feel like for its human operatives. There is consensus among historians and sociologists of the computer that the first personal computers were developed for hobbyists and enthusiasts by hobbyists and enthusiasts,[1] although there is less agreement on the significance that should be attached to this. Ceruzzi's (2000) definitive history of Twentieth Century computing notes that the hobbyist culture took the lead in exploiting the rapid improvements in integrated circuitry associated with the rise of the 'micro-chip'. Neither chip producers nor computer manufacturers saw any market for small interactive computers that might be marketed to private individuals (Freiberger and Swaine 1984: 58; Ceruzzi 2000: 223-4). Purchasers of the Altair had to understand how to build the machine out of an assortment of mechanical bits and pieces (Levy 1984: 191-3; Ceruzzi 2000: 226). These included a tiny processor, a small memory and limited input/output capabilities – there was no screen, just an array of lights, and no keyboard (Freiberger and Swaine 1984: 38). The poverty of this interface makes these early machines barely recognisable, from a contemporary perspective, as PCs. The screen, which defined the 'play-space' of the PDP-10, the machine on which the first computer game was made, does not

---

[1] Comments to this effect can be found in Ceruzzi (2000); Freiberger and Swaine (1984); Goldberg (1988); Levy (1984); Pfaffenberger (1988); Raymond (1999), and throughout the sociological literature on computing and the cultural impact of computers.

seem to have been integral to the PC idea at this stage. The people who wanted PCs in 1975 did not want to play games, they wanted to hack.

In this chapter I will draw an analogy between the hacker pioneers of personal computing and the seventeenth century Protestant sects described by Weber in his *The Protestant Ethic and the Spirit of Capitalism* (1974). This analogy clarifies the relationship between hackers and 'informational capitalism' (defined below) and facilitates a measured understanding of the historic role of the original hackers and the sociological significance of contemporary hacking. Weber's book is a piece of historical sociology, in which he emphasises that the Protestant ethic was itself *not* pro-capitalist (1974: 89). He describes the historical irony that it fed into the development of capitalism and that this system generated social outcomes which were profoundly deleterious to the spirit of Protestantism. Using analogy with Weber's argument to explore the role of the hacker pioneers in the history of personal computing facilitates a critical perspective on the information society and its technological basis, the networked PC. The hackers and their ethics occupy a similarly ambiguous and contradictory relationship to the development of capitalist society to that held by Weber's historical Protestants. Hackers should not be deified as romantic rebels, nemeses of networked capitalism, nor relegated to a footnote in the history of personal computing. Examining their attitudes and beliefs in connection with the personal computer furnishes us with the basis for a critical perspective on the diffusion of personal computers and other intelligent artefacts. Like the Protestants of early modern Europe, the American PC enthusiasts of the 1960s and 1970s founded a new and distinctive worldview. This worldview profoundly saturated the existence of the PC pioneers, moulding their experience of the world in a way that is thoroughly comparable to the impact on the members of the seventeenth century Protestant sects of their religious beliefs. Moreover, just as Protestantism has been assigned a fundamental explanatory role in the development of modern capitalism, so the worldview of the PC pioneers has been objectively significant for the shape of world history since the 1970s and 1980s.

I begin by developing the analogy between the Protestants and the hacker sub-culture of the 1960s and 1970s. Both groups valued intense diligence, rational thought and constant reflection as keys to personal virtue. Both emphasised these qualities over more conventional indicators of the moral quality of one's character and behaviour – such as kindness. While they each assumed that their new beliefs would augur positive changes in society at large, this was the priority for neither of them – their primary orientation was solitary and inward. Both bequeathed to society a powerful basis for the quickening of capitalist modernisation processes, though neither could be said to have intended this outcome and its effects were deleterious for the belief and value systems of both groups.

From the late 1980s onwards the PC came to occupy a pivotal role in the development of the economic, or systems sphere of society. In the process, the PC was transformed from an austere, demanding machine into something 'friendly' and 'easy to use'. In the second section I argue that this kind of PC has become socially ubiquitous principally because it is the form of computer technology that is most consistent with the interests of key economic players. The impact of the new technology has led some to argue that we are now living in a new mode of production: 'informationalism', or 'informational capitalism'. This new economy presupposes that computers' processing power is easily available to individual workers. The discrepancy between computers as they were conceived by radical hackers, and modern PCs is found to be consistent with the central analogy being drawn by the paper. Just as in capitalism consumption supplants religion as the basis for the diffusion of the work ethic, so in informationalism the interface displaces the hackers' reasons for engaging with technology and replaces them with the promise of an aesthetic, pleasing experience.

In Habermas's reading of Weber, the notion of an ironic, historical disenchantment of the Protestants' beliefs is particularly emphasised. This emphasis motivates the analogy with the PC hackers, since the fate of their vision has been conspicuously similar. Just as *religious* Protestantism created the juridico-legal and subjective psychological context for the emergence of an utterly *secular* social system, so the computer-loving hackers created the technological foundation of a society in which human enthusiasm for and mastery of advanced technology is ironically negated. In the rest of this chapter I argue that these pioneers of personal computing were similar to the Protestants of early modern Europe. The similarities encompass the psychology of individual members of each group; their social (or anti-social) priorities, and, ultimately, their historic function in inaugurating a new kind of society. The point of such a parallel is to explore the significance of hacking as a source of critical perspectives on computer technology, and the usefulness of this orientation towards the machine to the development of a design critique of the PC interface. This is a very different project from that of identifying hackers as 'techno-rebels' or 'hacktivists', a topic to which I return in later chapters. In conclusion, this chapter argues that the analogy is useful for the development of a critical sociology of the contemporary PC – the goal of subsequent chapters. The mode of presentation of PCs and other artefacts needs to be checked by a more cautious, circumspect, and critical approach to the social context of interface design.

The Hacker Sub-Culture and the PC Idea

As Sherry Turkle has pointed out, the seductions of contemporary personal computing are very different from those which appealed to the hacker pioneers. Modern PC users are attracted by beautiful screen imagery and sumptuous multi-medic environments. As we will see in the next chapter, the modern PC comes wrapped in a rhetoric about 'virtuality' and an ideology of 'exploration'. Early enthusiasts of the PC were not captivated by the interface as we are, however. They were not held in thrall to graphical, animated, sound-enabled light shows. For them,

> What would come out of these systems was not as important as the act of understanding, explaining and changing the systems themselves... (Levy 1984: 192)

In other words, although the idea of a playful machine that is interactive and supports a virtual environment seems essential to what we mean by personal computing today, the appeal of the first computers lay elsewhere, namely in the intense, abstract and methodical reasoning that the computer demanded of its human users. This attitude towards computing characterised what Levy calls the 'hardware hackers' of the 1960s and 1970s. They were a loosely affiliated group, perhaps numbering only a few thousand people distributed across the US, who pioneered the development of personal computers. Similarly, while we tend to understand the dispute between 'hackers' and orthodox computer scientists in terms of such issues as privacy, intellectual property rights and so on, the first hackers antagonised the computing establishment for slightly different reasons. The 'hackers' of this period were remarkable less for their cavalier approach towards other people's machines and files but because of their attitudes to and beliefs about computers; their desire to see others use computers, and their distinctive way of interacting with the machines.

A Life Guided by Constant Thought

Just like the early Protestants (Weber 1974: 137), hackers set a positive moral value on diligence. It was not possible to be esteemed as a bona fide enthusiast without putting in the hours. Exceptional single-mindedness and determination to keep plugging away at a problem until the optimal solution had been found are well-documented traits of the early hackers, in accounts of the MIT hackers and of the PC pioneers proper. Willingness to work right through the night on a single programming problem are widely cited as features of the early 'hacker' computer culture (Levy 1984: 35, 84-5, 220; Turkle 1984: 207; Weizenbaum 1976: 117; Chandler 1996: 230). The psychology of those who 'personalised' computing in the 1970s was one of devotion to abstract reasoning and intense concentration and not the joys of real-time interactivity.

As will be seen in chapter five, this love of working with the technology for its own sake perhaps defines the hacker's attitude to computers to this day. It aligns the pioneers with the Protestants who, while making legitimate acquisition of wealth socially acceptable, did not allow themselves its pleasures and insisted that work should be motivated by its virtuous character and not its material rewards (Weber 1974: 68, 137). For hackers, the computer came to feel like an extension of themselves. They experienced a sense of 'fusion' with the machine (Levy 1984: 218) and perhaps even started to 'think' in programming language. In this sense, they were absorbed in an on-going dialogue with the machine, but the dialogue metaphor should not be strained.[2] The holding power of early PCs had more the

---

[2] Habermas (1979: 81-90) rejects Marcuse's utopian vision of a harmonious integration of society and nature on the grounds that it would entail communication with physical objects, which is impossible. Feenberg (1999: 153-4) argues that this is a kind of dogmatism on Habermas's part. On the account developed here, our interaction with objects perceived as technical has some but not all of the features of a communicative exchange.

character of an extended experiment than a natural conversation. Hypothesis, deliberation and calculation were the protracted precursors to getting a machine response. The experience of using an Altair 8800 was much more like trying to build your own radio set than 'interacting' with a modern PC.

Sherry Turkle noted that this intense engagement with the PC could sometimes become a trap (1984: 214). People who lacked social skills could be drawn into a relationship with the machine that would impair their psychological development and inhibit both their capacity and desire to understand others. In terms of developmental psychology, people who were trapped in this way would probably be best described as locked into what developmental psychologists call the 'traditional' stage of moral development – they were rigorous rule followers. For hackers, working with the computer became an undemanding substitute for human companionship: 'The hacker culture,' Turkle writes, '…is a culture of loners who are never alone' (1984: 219). These people had evolved a kind of co-existence in which no one judged anyone else, but no one took much interest in anyone else either. Levy makes similar observations about the MIT hackers, who seem to have walked a line between virtuous toleration and mutual indifference bordering on the callous. All of which echoes Weber's comments on the profound loneliness of the Protestant sectarians and on their individualism (1974: 104, 106). A climate of moral indifference to one another characterised the 'obsessive' wing of the computer culture in the 1970s and early 1980s. It is completely consistent with the ethos of early Protestantism, in its individualism and its emphasis on toleration.

Pekka Himanen likens the intense engagement with the machine that characterises hacking with the obsessive play of computer gamers. This leads him to suggest that, 'The original meanings of the terms *capitalist* and *hacker* pull in different directions' (2001: 36). While capitalism promotes the work ethic, he argues, hackers played with machines for fun. This reading overlooks Weber's own view that the Protestant ethic was not overtly 'pro-capitalist'. At the same time, Himanen conflates two aspects of the psychology of engagement with computers – the attitude of intense concentration and abstract reasoning on one side and that of playful interactivity within a virtual world on the other. This approach obscures much of what is useful in the hacking attitude when it comes to developing a design critique of contemporary PC technology and implies a political critique of capitalism that targets the seriousness of life under that system, something which will strike many as misplaced. Himanen also argues that the intensity and passion of hacker activity turns on social recognition: 'For hackers, …the basic organisational factor in life is not work or money but passion and the desire to create something socially valuable together' (Himanen 2001: 53).[3] This assertion seems to be based on his knowledge of Linus Torvald's work on the LINUX operating system, rather than the hackers who laid the foundations for the information society by pioneering the development of personal computing. It overlooks the intensely solitary nature of what those hackers actually had to do in order to achieve anything. According to Weizenbaum, even a short program could

---

[3] Himanen claims that hacker unsociability is a myth (2001: 52).

take between twenty and thirty hours to write for the machines of that period. He observed that the hackers in his faculty would '...not converse with anyone but the computer' (1976: 118, 120). It is not, of course strictly accurate to say that they were conversing with the machine, but the observation is highly suggestive.

Computers have always tended to isolate the people who use them – a fact that is implicitly acknowledged by Himanen elsewhere (2001: 134). We do not need to project an ideal of sociability back onto the PC pioneers in order to excavate the radical potential in their world view. All the evidence suggests that they were not interested in other people, being given over instead to a kind of immersion in the machine, itself mediated not by sumptuous screen imagery and simulations but by rational thought. Moreover, just as being theologically learned was, for the seventeenth century sects, no proof of one's elect status (Weber 1974: 129) so paper qualifications, even in computer science were also no substitute for what was known as the 'hands-on' principle, even at MIT (Levy 1984: 157-8; Freiberger and Swaine 1984: 22). What mattered in early hacker culture was making programs that worked.

Turkle reports that the members of this culture allowed each other a 'great deal of psychological space'. In this space, idiosyncracies were allowed to develop which, in other social contexts, might have incurred negative peer judgements. Levy and Weizenbaum both describe hackers as unwashed, dishevelled, socially inept to the point of rudeness, and uniquely oblivious to other peoples' feelings. One of Levy's hackers is described as announcing one day that he had decided to get married, though upon further questioning it turned out that the lucky woman had not yet been identified (Levy 1984: 86). In a similar way, Weber describes the Protestants as having supplanted a compassionate attitude towards others with a judgemental one. For the pioneers, it seems that the computer plays the role of God, whose requirements took priority over the more conventional ones of sentiment when it came to assessing one's duty to others (Weber 1974: 226 fn 34).

Like the early Protestants, the hacker pioneers prioritised rule following, methodical conduct over pleasure. What pleasures they would allow themselves were of a purely cerebral nature, such as the thrill of getting 'the right solution' to a programming problem. This has much more to do with the 'ecstatic bliss', which some Protestants conceived as the absolute antithesis to sensual indulgence (Weber 1974: 119, 139, 151) than social recognition. Indeed, there is perhaps even an analogy with recognition of the 'elect' in the Protestant sects, which was a thoroughly secondary feature of actually being elect.

The pioneers placed such emphasis on understanding the machine level because only such an understanding could truly empower the computer user; frippery and extravagance would divert his[4] attention from what was really going on in the machine. Investing their understanding of logical detail with moral connotations, the computer pioneers revitalised an idea that we associate with Kant, namely, the notion of autonomy as living in accordance with the demands of reason. The effort to comprehend the machine level became a living analogy with

---

[4] Hacking has always been an almost exclusively male activity. I do not attempt to explain this here. For interesting discussion of the issue, see Turkle (1984).

the Enlightenment's moral injunction to become autonomous by following one's own reason, rather than bowing to convention. This ideal is the key to the aspirations and beliefs that the pioneers shared in relation to computers. For them, the computer was a means of encouraging people to live a 'life guided by constant thought' (Weber 1974: 118). If other people could be persuaded to engage with the machine in its glorious, digital-logical complexity then they too might be empowered. The computer offered opportunities for,

> ...the act of creation, the benevolent exercise of power in the logical, unambiguous world of computers where truth, openness and democracy existed in a form purer than one could find anywhere else. (Levy 1984: 192)[5]

Ultimately, coming to understand the machine offers the human being a sense of personal empowerment. This folk technology was the guiding orientation of hackers as they struggled to codify computer technology in a form that would put it at the disposal of each human individual.

Hackers were parsimonious in their attitude towards the machine's resources. They esteemed only the 'best' programming solutions because these represented the most economic use of the computer's limited capabilities. Initially, this was probably a function of the limited resources available. But as components became more powerful and cheaply available throughout the 1980s and the computer culture spread beyond its sub-cultural origins parsimony continued to be a part of the hacker, or hard-core enthusiast, ethos. Where other hobbyists might have settled for programs that worked, hackers wanted programs that were elegant and efficient. Their search for new functions required that they minimise expenditure of the computer's memory and processing power. Hours of experimentation and frustration in pursuit of a solution would be followed by yet more tortuous hours refining it and making it the best one possible. For them, the effort of achieving this strange perfection was more important even than the function or effect being worked on. The PC pioneers would eschew wasteful solutions (programs that used more lines of code than was strictly necessary, for example) or exaggerated effects, as these separated users from the machine level (Levy 1984: 43; similar observations, though not cast in these terms, can be found in Weizenbaum (1976: 120).

Once again, this prompts comparison with Weber's Protestants, who famously renounced ritual and symbolism in favour of the methodical conduct that was virtuous living. They despised theatre and conspicuous public displays of colour, because such activities were distractions from God (Weber 1974: 104-6, 169). This emphasis on austerity, an ethos of refusing to be concerned with the inessential, conflicts with Himanen's thesis that hackers placed great emphasis on working

---

[5] Freiberger and Swaine refer to 'the clean edge of the logic and *the fairness of the game* of programming' (1984, 23 my emphasis), as fundamental to its addictiveness.

hard in order to make time for play (2001: 26).[6] Himanen suggests that they were particularly interested in writing and playing computer games and this may well have been true. But there is little evidence that playing games was the coveted reward or incentive for the activity of programming. Most accounts, including Himanen's own, stress the importance to hackers of programming as a desirable activity itself. Torvalds, in his preface to Himanen's book, makes the distinction clear when he says that, for hackers, the behaviour of the computer is intrinsically entertaining, *not* games and *not* the 'pretty pictures on the Internet' (Himanen 2001: *xvii*). The hacker enthusiasm for writing games reflects the fact that computer and PC technology had entered a phase in their development during which 'solutions' outnumbered problems. Thomas Hughes and others (in Bijker *et al* 1989) have shown that such phases are common in the history of technology. Their intense, intellectual engagement with computer technology and their desire to see this extended to other people underscore the hackers' goal of personal computing and not their interest in playing games.[7]

Computer Power to the People

Like Weber's Protestants, the computer pioneers were certainly not 'pro-capitalist' and there is even evidence that some of them understood their beliefs in relation to the computer as implying a degree of opposition to that social system. Their technological aspirations were sometimes expressed in anti-capitalist terms, and this was not exclusively to do with issues that we understand as motivating contemporary 'hackers' – copyright, software piracy, and so on. It would also be wrong to identify a sense of play, or opposition to the modern day 'work ethic' as defining their oppositional stance. The radicalism of the hacker pioneers was much more serious than this and seems to have been largely obscured by subsequent events. Their idea was that computers would make people more autonomous while at the same time making more information available to more people. The outcome of such a fortuitous combination could surely only be progressive, perhaps even revolutionary. In attempting to codify computer technology as 'personal' by so concatenating technical elements as to place information processing power within the control of the human individual, the PC hackers contested corporate and state control of computer technology and advocated a design consistent with radical democracy.

It is important at this point to place the hackers in the context of 1960s youth culture. The project of appropriating computer technology and making it

---

[6] Ceruzzi makes a similar claim when he writes that, 'the first thing they did with the[se] machines, once they got them running, was play games' (2000: 230). This is strange as he is unwilling to generalise about other hacker traits, arguing that, 'there was no such thing as a typical member of the Homebrew Computer Club...' (2000: 216), for example.
[7] Neither Weizenbaum (1976) nor Turkle (1984) even mention games playing in their contemporaneous accounts of the original hackers. They are also not mentioned in Freiberger and Swain's (1984) study of the early history of personal computing.

accessible to individuals could probably not have taken root in any other situation. The hackers were a sub-culture within the 1960s counter-culture, which was concerned to challenge the prevailing deference to technological expertise. According to Theodore Roszack's seminal account, the hippies and students of 1960s America were attempting to challenge a society in which, '...the citizen, confronted by bewildering bigness and complexity, finds it necessary to defer on all matters to those who know better' (1968: 7). From the point of view of most radicalised youth, technology had created a situation in which power was invested in large, centralised structures that could only be understood by experts (Roszack 1968: 206). This overweening system placed the role of values in human affairs in jeopardy. The hippy revolution was supposed to overturn the 'machine'. In this context, the hackers clearly occupied a paradoxical position. They were young, looked and smelled like hippies, and were at home in the milieu just described. And yet, far from being opposed to technology, they were fixated on it. What they seem to have glimpsed was the possibility of overturning technology's bigness and its centralisation in the hands of the powerful, without losing its power to liberate. In other words, they saw the possibility of giving computer power to ordinary people as a weapon that might actually undermine the authority of the expert and the hold of the monolithic system. Herbert Marcuse had called for qualitative social change of an order that '...would alter the direction of technical progress – that is, develop a new technology' (1964: 227). The hackers may not all have read his words, but they answered the call.

Feenberg's remarks on 1968 contextualise this attempt to appropriate technology. Analysing the student revolts of that year and focusing particularly on the French case, he asks why young, middle class people in wealthy societies took to the streets in the name of revolution. His answer is that, while modern societies produce wealth and patterns of wealth distribution that benefit educated elites, nonetheless the technocratic nature of those societies creates frustration and dissatisfaction:

> The students found themselves at the leading edge of a contradiction that cuts across all modern societies, the contradiction between the enormous knowledge and wealth of those societies and the creativity they demand of their members, and the mediocre use to which this knowledge, wealth and creativity is put. And they believed they had a solution to the problem in a transformation of the place of knowledge – and their own future role – in the social structure (Feenberg 1999: 26).

The students wanted to end technocracy, abolishing the division of labour between manual and professional work, eliminating the prevailing culture of deference to expertise and doing away with distinctions of social class. This was the social context in which the hacker pioneers contested computer technology and came up with their own form of it.

Some hackers wanted computers that would realize Ivan Illich's ideal of 'tools for conviviality' and facilitate community based education networks (Illich 1979). The Community Memory Project is a particularly good example. The project set up a proto-terminal with a cardboard shell in a record shop. Essentially an evolving database, the computer allowed people to enter information about themselves and to search for things, people and services they were interested in. It quickly attracted large numbers of people and vindicated the pioneers' notion that, '...the very presence of computers in accessible places might be a spur for social change, a chance to see the possibilities opened up by new technology' (Levy 1984: 179). For some of the pioneers the political radicalism of the Community Memory Project was overt and explicit. Others were, perhaps, drawn by a more vague sense that the computer could be a kind of material support for a society based on co-operation and community. The radical aspirations of the computer pioneers and their self-identification with the hippy counterculture are clear from the names of their associations and publications. The 'People's Computer Company' (PCC), for instance, was named with ironic reference to a Janis Joplin album and similar undertones can be discerned in the name of the Stanford based 'Homebrew' computer club. The club produced a publication of the same name which carried articles inciting people to get involved in computing and to determine the shape of the technological future. One of PCC's associates was Ted Nelson, whose views on interface design we will return to in the next chapter, author of a book entitled 'Computer Lib' and of the slogan, 'Computer Power to the People!' (cited in Levy 1984: 169). Similarly, Steve Wozniak, also a member of the Homebrew computer club, has been quoted as saying that he came from a 'group of beatniks or hippies' who 'were going to totally change the world' (in Himanen 2001: 188).

The hackers invested their hopes for social transformation in the PC, in much the same way that more numerous people placed similar ideological investments in pharmaceuticals. Timothy Leary's call for a 'revolution of the central nervous system' through mass consumption of LSD was no less dependent upon Twentieth Century science. Roszack argued that, ironically, this made the drugs culture essentially continuous with the middle class mainstream:

> The gadget happy American has always been a figure of fun because of his facile assumption that there exists a technological solution to every human problem. It only took the great psychedelic crusade to perfect the absurdity by proclaiming that personal salvation and the social revolution can be packed in a capsule. (Roszack 1968: 177)

These remarks could have been applied with even greater irony to the hacker sub-group.[8] Nonetheless, the radicalism of their ideological investments in the machine and the influence of the counter-cultural context on their beliefs should not be overlooked in attempts to comprehend the history of the information age.

While the pioneers were evangelical about their machines, we also should not exaggerate the extent to which their aspirations in connection with them were conceived in overtly social or political terms. As Roszack emphasises, a significant

---

[8] Wozniak's comment (above) also makes him 'decadent' on Roszack's definition (1968: 270), because he appears to invest hopes for social transformation in one potentially trivial object, rather than displaying an engagement with broader social and political questions on their own terms.

feature of the 1960s counter-culture generally was its subjectivism; its capacity for transforming political questions into psychological ones. Most hackers simply wanted people to use computers and seem to have assumed that the consequences of such a diffusion of the technology would be benign. Again, this mirrors the attitude of the Protestants, who, Weber tells us, were not interested in projects of social reform. Their only concern was with the saving of souls (Weber 1974: 89). Whatever the radical aspirations of the pioneers of personal computing, they depended for their realization upon the development of computers that were sufficiently powerful and accessible and a human population that would be willing to learn to use them. As Lee Felsenstein emphasised in 1975:

> The convivial approach I suggest would rely on the user's ability to learn about and gain some control over the tool. The user will have to spend some amount of time probing around inside the equipment, and we will have to make this possible and not fatal to either the equipment or the person. (cited in Levy 1984: 238)

Felsenstein's anxiety was that the PC revolution should be carried through by machines that allowed people to experiment, to find out for themselves how computers worked. He saw that people who did not understand computers would be at a fundamental disadvantage when it came to living in a society based on extensive computer use. The ideal of machine transparency was fundamental to the experience of autonomy that could be had through interaction with a computer. As the Protestants stressed the importance of reading the Bible for oneself, so hackers argued that people could not be empowered by the machine if they did not know how it worked. Transparency was also intrinsic to the use of the computer as a convivial tool; a means of identifying others with similar interests, communicating with them and co-ordinating activities with them. A situation where everyone could not do this equally well could be socially exclusive. The implications for democracy of inequalities of access to the machine would be profoundly regressive. Felsenstein and his comrades denounced the idea that computers could be built for use by people who did not understand their inner workings as the philosophy of 'Design by geniuses for use by idiots' (Quoted in Levy, 1984: 238).

There is an important distinction to be drawn here between hacker purists who enjoyed the intellectual challenge of early PCs and those who perceived early on the potential allure of interactivity within a computer-supported virtual environment. That there was an implicit tension between the two even at this early stage in the history of personal computing is illustrated by the relationship between Steve Wozniak and Steve Jobs. They made the first Apple PC and, in 1977, the Apple II, which was the first commercial PC to have a seductive graphical interface using a colour monitor. Jobs worked in the games industry and is widely acknowledged to have been an inspirational innovator in design and marketing. Wozniak was a hacker and is, by reputation, a brilliant programmer who came up with the architecture of the Apple PC. Both played games, but according to Steve Kent, Wozniak was the technologically gifted member of the team and would spend long hours working on programming problems, while Jobs's talents lay more in the field of visionary design and marketing. Industry rumour, reported by Kent, has it that Jobs exploited his less socially aware friend (Kent 2001: 72-3). Whether this is true or not, the story is suggestive because within a few years of the emergence of a graphical user interface on mass-produced PCs the radical implications of personal computing as conceived by the hacker pioneers were being negated. Graphical interfaces ensured that PCs were transformed into tools for pleasure rather than enlightenment – the biggest selling PC of the early 1980s was the Commodore 64, which was widely perceived as a games console. Austerity was giving way to indulgence.

Social Selection and the Development of the PC Idea

Ceruzzi writes that 'The assertion that hackers created modern interactive computing is about half right' (2000: 215) and argues that they, '...provided an infrastructure of support...' (2000: 224) which was essential to the development of the PC as a viable commodity. They were also responsible for key innovations in the development of the technology, such as the use of keyboards as input devices and television screens for output (2000: 231). Even Weizenbaum, who took a very negative view of the hackers he encountered in the 1960s and 1970s, grudgingly acknowledged that, '...were it not for the often, in its terms, highly creative labor of people who proudly claim the title 'hacker,' few of today's sophisticated computer time-sharing systems, computer language translators, computer graphics systems, etc., would exist' (1976: 119). Sherry Turkle acknowledges that '...hackers play a significant, though controversial role in the history of computation' (1984: 210). However, the role of the hackers cannot simply be reduced to the role of individuals whose inventions contributed to the functional diversification and improvements in the performance of the technology. The PC was an experimental manifestation of computing as a social practice as much as it was the outcome of technical progress. Moreover, it was a social experiment that no large computer manufacturers viewed with any great enthusiasm. Personal computing seemed, in the 1970s, unlikely to be anything more than a minority pursuit. What changed this was the realization by key players in the economic system that personalising the experience of using a computer was the best way for them to exploit the potential benefits of the technology. This converged with the gradual discovery of an accessible, captivating 'world' at the screen, which began to eclipse the perspective and aspirations of the 'Protestant' hackers.

The Social Transformation of the PC

Just as the Protestants contributed to the emergence of a legal and ethical context that was peculiarly conducive to capitalist accumulation, so the hackers' ideal – personal computing – has enabled capitalism to exploit computer technology. As late as 1984, David Burnham (1984, 88-9) observed that the full range of information processing techniques were still not available to individual computer users. It was only when this situation was changed that the new, 'informational spirit' could take over. The use of PCs in the construction of the networked capitalist economy is so extensive that it seems to have realized the hacker ideal of ubiquitous computing. However, most users of PCs in the informational economy do not have the hacker love of computers. The appropriation of PCs by key players in the economic system and the social diffusion of PCs more generally since the late 1980s, have been expedited by the development of machine interfaces that do not allow the kind of exploration and experimentation so valued by the early hackers. In place of the hacker ideal of empowerment through struggle with the digital-logical complexities of the machine, we find an altogether more pragmatic model of user empowerment articulated in the work of interface designers.[9]

Before the early 1990s, in the computer culture, interface design was considered trivial (Laurel 1993: 48), even 'sissy' (Negroponte 1995: 90) compared to the rigours of hardware engineering or mathematically informed programming. The hackers who dominated that culture were intolerant of lazy people who would not work to gain control over the machine and viewed attempts to make computers more accessible as wasteful. Just as the sectarian Protestants viewed sin not as a reminder of their own moral vulnerabilities and weakness, as in traditional Christianity, but as evidence of the damned status of the sinner (Weber 1974: 122), so hackers were highly disparaging of the technically inept. Nicholas Negroponte, an early advocate of the 'friendly' interface, describes his struggle against elements within the computer culture in suitably religious terms:

> In my opinion there was a subconscious effort to keep it [computing] mysterious, like the monopoly of the monks, or some bizarre religious rite in the Dark Ages. (1995: 90)

Similarly, Steven Johnson refers to the anti-graphical interface attitude of DOS programmers as a kind of 'snobbery' (1997: 58), while Turkle describes purist advocates of the older, command line interfaces as members of an 'epistemological elite' (1996: 54). From the mid-1980s, then, emphasis on transparency, austere interface design and the importance of understanding the machine as a machine, all fundamental to the hacker worldview, began to be derided as the elitist perspective of 'engineers' – a much less glamorous term.

In their struggle to transform the PC, the interface specialists eventually won out over this so-called 'priesthood', although there is little sense of how this victory was achieved in the sources just cited. As we will see in the next chapter, the guiding principle of modern interface design is that the ordinary PC user does not need to know what is going on inside the machine in order to feel empowered by using it. A user can experience a sense of being in control without being challenged by the computer and without having to respond by thinking hard about

---

[9] Ben Schneidermann, for instance, a leading interface design theorist writes that users '...strongly desire *the sense* that they are in charge of the system...' (1997: 75, my emphasis). Similar comments can be found in Preece *et al* (1998, 310). Interface design ideology is the subject of the next chapter.

how it works. Instead, empowerment is now defined in terms of the user's ability to achieve practical goals that have nothing to do with computing. According to Turkle (1996: 61) even computer programming no longer requires an understanding of the detailed workings of the machine.[10] A standard part of a Java programmer's work, for instance, is the importation of files that provide services for the program they are working on at the time and which are publicly available over the Internet. The contemporary programmer is cutting and pasting, albeit it at quite a technical level, rather than probing the depths of the machine. Even quite complex software engineering problems have been made 'easy' (I use the word advisedly) by the development of special applications which to some extent write the code for the user.[11]

The PCs that the vast majority of people use come with interfaces that actually deny them access to the underlying machine. Instead of the austerity esteemed by the hackers, colours, sounds and pictures are all deployed to render the experience of using a computer pleasurable and unchallenging. Without having to acquire any programming knowledge, users can manipulate these variables to their own tastes. It is through the medium of this interface that the PC has been inserted into almost every conceivable social location during the last decade. This 'seductive' interface (Turkle 1996) is radically at odds with the parsimonious computational aesthetic of the computer pioneers. It builds on the principle of computer gaming that the computer offers us a self-contained world of fantastic experiences, a realm where our actions can be both unproductive and yet legitimate – an escape from the normal rigours of adult life.[12] In this way, the PC is now associated with a diffusion of 'play' type experiences into various domains of life and work. It allows users to indulge themselves in a way that is wasteful with regard to memory and processing power. This interface is seductive in the fullest sense, however, being both attractive and deceitful. As Brenda Laurel points out (1993: 105), the user of a modern PC encounters an environment full of implicit rather than explicit constraints and obstacles. Instead of inviting people to discover the 'pure democracy' of the machine, the PC now presents as something other than a machine – as a 'person or a new town' (Turkle 1996: 23); as a new kind of novel (Johnson 1997), or even as a form of theatre (Laurel 1993). This deception of the user is, perhaps, harmless enough. It is, however, deeply implicated in the process whereby the economic system has been able to capitalise on the PC idea. The

---

[10] This is certainly an exaggeration on Turkle's part. Contemporary programming languages, such as Java, have elements in their syntax that are almost 'natural' in their relation to the effects they can produce. The command 'system.out.println', for instance, will tell the machine to generate the line of text that follows it as output to the computer screen when this point in the program has been reached. There remains, however, an enormous difference between writing a program in Java and composing an essay in natural language, or even reading a map.

[11] If we consider HTML a programming language, then web authoring tools like 'FrontPage' do this. A better example, though less well known, is the 'Rational Rose' program which is used in the software engineering industry.

[12] On this definition of play, see Caillois (1958: 9, 10).

implicit constraints that are written into the program interface are carefully calibrated to ensure that the user is guided by the application she is using to the successful accomplishment of a predetermined task. The hacker ideal of achieving *true* mastery is neutralised by the 'easy to use' interface, which embodies a prohibition on the very kind of thinking that was so important to the hacker pioneers of personal computing.

The ideals and aspirations of a radical sub-culture were, as we have seen, embodied in the PC. It mediated their aspirations, carrying them to the broader society. But in the process, the machine itself has been mediated and transformed into something quite different. Just as the individualist, disciplined and diligent ethos of the Protestant sects infused and energised early capitalism, so the social spread of the PC has revolutionised contemporary social relations. However, as capitalism created the conditions under which religious belief seems increasingly anachronistic, so the modern PC is not any longer the kind of object that the pioneers envisaged as the bearer of their socially progressive ideals. The re-aestheticisation of technology envisaged by Feenberg and the class of '68 has certainly brought about social and cultural transformations, but these were not associated with social progress or the hoped for negation of capitalism.

Systems Level Appropriation of the PC

The social constructionist scholar, Thomas Hughes distinguishes radical from conservative technological innovations in the following way:

> Inventions can be conservative or radical. Those occurring during the inventive phase are radical because they inaugurate a new system; conservative inventions predominate during the phase of competition and system growth, for they improve or expand existing systems. (In Bijker *et al* 1989: 57)

The PC was radical technology. It inaugurated a new economic era in which production and distribution processes were accelerated. As the interface has grown in sophistication, however, the PC has been used to enhance management control over these processes, and to 'steer' the actions of human operatives at all levels. Interfaces that conceal the underlying, technical aspects of the machine stymie and inhibit shop-floor innovation and reduce the likelihood of further, hacker-style, experimentation with PC technology. In this way, the PC helps consolidate and stabilise social relations. The PC idea has been selectively retained[13] by the social system in much the same way that Protestant ideas were used to restructure the legal systems of early capitalism. In the aestheticisation of the PC rational deliberation has been displaced by the needs of money and power in determining the form taken by the technology.

---

[13] The role of selection as a concept in contemporary critical theory of social evolution is discussed in Esteban (1991).

The idea of personal computing – placing the power of the computer at the disposal of each individual – was intended to contribute to what Habermas calls 'progressive rationalisation' of the cultural lifeworld. Its pioneers envisaged the PC as an agent of autonomy; of empowerment through the use of reason. However, the computer power that has been devolved to the level of the individual work-station has been carefully designed to limit workers' access to it. This partial implementation of the idea of personal computing ensures that it contributes not to the rationalisation of work-place culture in a progressive sense, but to efficiency gains in the economic system. It is in the context of a critical understanding of how the two dimensions of social evolution interact that we can grasp the social implications of the PC. The irony in Weber's historical thesis is the classic illustration of such a critical understanding at work.

Modern corporations use the computer's information processing power to identify patterns and regularities that represent opportunities for more effective business performance. It is now possible, for instance, to source the cheapest supplier of any part for any manufacturing process world-wide in a matter of moments.[14] Such information gathering is vital to competitiveness. The rapid spread of computer technology and its use to carry out this kind of activity has altered the focus of economic practice all over the world. The scale of this change and its qualitative impact in reshaping production processes has led some to argue that we now live in a new mode of production – informationalism.[15] Michael Carnoy, for instance, writes that:

> Production in the advanced capitalist societies shifts from material goods to information-processing activities, fundamentally changing the structure of these societies to favour economic activities that focus on symbol manipulation in the organisation of production and in the enhancement of productivity. (Carnoy *et al* 1995: 5)

These changes have also been associated with a significant increase in the rate of profit (Castells 1996: 85). By placing the information processing power of the PC at the disposal of individual workers, capital has been able fully to exploit the possibilities of the computer revolution. Every worker is 'networked' and plays his or her part in the flow of information that makes possible flexible, optimal, 'just-in-time' responses to dynamic global situations.

Castells and Carnoy maintain that work in this economy requires more sophistication and a higher degree of education than was widely available under previous forms of capitalism. In fact, though, the interface has been designed to relieve the worker of 'cognitive burdens' associated with real computing. As Perelman points out, spending on public education in the developed world has actually fallen in the informational era and in some areas the authorities are spending more on prisons than they do on schools (Perelman 1998: 25-27). Most

---

[14] Similarly, data on consumers' behaviour can be collated and searched to establish more efficient ways of classifying and targeting markets.

[15] See Castells (1996: 95).

contemporary work with computers is dull and routine. This dramatically negates the hacker ideal of autonomy through enlightenment gained from working with the PC.[16]

The interface also relieves employers of the need to train employees in the proper use of the technology. 'User friendly' applications enable the modern firm to perform any number of information processing practices without hiring experts or training staff. The diffusion of networked PCs, or 'informationalisation' has been instrumental in creating conditions of endemic job insecurity (Greider 1997: 28, 16-121; Klein 1999: 242-4; Perelman 1998: 56). Computer databases contain the knowledge that is essential to company performance, knowledge that used to be stored in workers' heads and was part of the 'informal culture' of organisations. As Mike Hales predicted, information processing technology 're-works the map of knowledge in the workplace' (1980: 142), actually limiting workers' discretion and reducing company reliance on employees' knowledge by subordinating everyone's actions to the imperatives expressed by the machine. The 'front end' of the application can be relied upon to 'operationalise' this knowledge by guiding the worker to successful completion of the task. The worker is intended to remain largely ignorant of the underlying mechanics throughout. By making such tasks 'easy' for the untrained worker, the new interfaces also represent a triumph of the endemic short-termism of contemporary capitalism – better trained employees would probably be able to achieve the same tasks and more with their powerful PCs.[17]

Messages that appear on the computer screen take on a kind of authority for the worker; they cannot be ignored and are likely to determine their subsequent actions.[18] This can be seen most clearly in service sector operations where employees find that they cannot give us what we ask for because 'the system' will not allow it. A number of studies have highlighted the role of the computer as a bearer of reified, symbolic significance in social space. Woolgar describes a process in which '...users have a configured relationship to... [the PC], such that only certain forms of access/use are encouraged' (in Law 1991: 89). Callaghan and Murphy (in Murphy *et al* 1989), argue that the computer serves to reinforce the notion of a single, oppressive reality that the worker must conform to at all costs. According to Kumar, computerisation extends the reach of Taylorism (Kumar 1995: 20), deepening its grip on those already subject to it and incorporating new layers of workers, including managers. As Michael Perelman writes,

---

[16] Pfaffenberger (1988) saw that hacker ideals were being negated in the practice of popular computing, but did not identify the changing nature of the machine as a factor in this – viewing it instead as the inevitable fate of all technology to serve power.

[17] I have suggested elsewhere that working in MS-DOS or UNIX environments can be more efficient, see Kirkpatrick 2000.

[18] Marcuse writes of the 'image' suppressing rational reflection on what to do next, as '...the technological veil conceals the reproduction of inequality and enslavement' (1964: 32) – at least a decade before the first Graphical User Interface.

While the modern information economy weakens the power of isolated individuals to understand, let alone assert their class interest, the same forces have been reinforcing the power of the ruling classes to wield class power. (Perelman 1998: 33)

The near ubiquity of PCs in the modern work place adds a whole new dimension to Marcuse's observation that, in high-tech economies '...ideology is in the process of production itself' (1964: 11). Put simply, the PC interface steers individual workers where their employers want them to go, while it conceals and withholds the social-transformative potential of the inner machine.

The 'friendly' interface allows even the most naïve user to relate to the global network of computer networks as if it were merely a large library – offering a nice, familiar little window for her search strings. As Steven Johnson points out (1997: 150), the interface acts as an information filter which sits between the user and the underlying programming and electronics and enables her to 'select' only that information that will be useful to her. Some kind of filtering role for the interface is probably a technical necessity because of the sheer quantity of data that is available on contemporary networks. The filtering process is also about social control, however. The vast majority of programs in industry are written 'in-house' (Raymond 1999) and, through them, corporations present their employees with the kind of information they want them to have and the kinds of decisions they want them to make.

Hard work, which was a Puritan virtue, had become for the people of Weber's time merely a necessity of life: 'The Puritan wanted to work in a calling: we are forced to do so' (1974: 181). This happened because the Protestant ethic transformed social relations, binding diligence and worldly success together. However, this transformation reacted back upon Protestantism itself. Work ceased to be 'virtuous' and became mundane, detached in the minds of those who had to do it from positive religious connotations. Protestantism, like all religions, became menaced by the atheistic ethos of capitalism. As John Wesley put it, '...although the form of religion remains, the spirit is swiftly vanishing away' (cited in Weber 1974: 175). Similarly, people are now obliged to use computers because of the pivotal place the machine holds in systems level processes. We develop competence in our work with computers for reasons that have nothing to do with the intellectual values of the hacker-pioneers. Under the guise of the friendly, controlling interface, the computer has become implicated in a paradoxical process of social rationalisation. While information flows more quickly and is processed more efficiently than ever before, heightening system flexibility and productiveness, people are actively discouraged from learning how their tools do this work and encouraged to relate to their machines as sources of a quasi-magical realm of play.

The hacker aspiration that everyone should use computers is close to being fulfilled in the rich countries of the world. However, this cannot be attributed to the radical ideas of the PC pioneers. Much as the Protestant ethic prepared the ground for the social acceptability of a more orderly, acquisitive orientation which was then transmitted by the success and spread of capitalism, so the PC has become socially diffuse as a consequence of its usefulness in streamlining contemporary economic and administrative processes. The radical spirit of the PC pioneers is a memory – in so far as it remains to haunt the modern PC user it is in the mythic figure of the 'hacker', or information pirate – while their basic article of faith has become mundane and uncontroversial.

Hacking and the Critical Theory of the PC

Habermas, in his reading of Weber, argues that Protestantism was a victim of what he calls '...the irresistible irony of the world-historical process of Enlightenment' (1995, 155). It would appear that a similar fate has befallen the benign worldview of the computer pioneers. The purpose of this attempt to clarify their perspectives, orientations and aspirations, however, has not been to advocate a return to the ideals of the PC pioneers. Transparency at every interface is neither attainable nor desirable if society is to benefit from computer technology. We should, moreover, be suspicious of attempts like Himanen's to eulogise the hacker and turn him into some sort of oppositional icon. However, if hackers' beliefs now seem somewhat anachronistic, they can form the basis for a critical and realist perspective on the whole question of how machines and human society mesh. Just as Kant expressed Protestant insights in a moral philosophy that speaks to secular concerns, so the hackers' ideals may be reworked as the basis of a critical perspective on computers and society.

The importance of recovering a sense of transparency as 'seeing the machine' lies in its realism. No one who uses a PC every day really believes that they are doing anything remotely like going to the theatre or talking to another person. When assessing the social impact of an interface we need to ask whether it facilitates the best possible use of computer resources. The truly empowered worker is one who can get the most out of his or her tools, not one who is seduced by them. At the same time, there are many social situations, especially in the systems sphere, wherein it will be objectively preferable for people to use technically opaque PCs – situations involving professionals who do not have time to become computer scientists, for instance. The interface is a heterogeneous phenomenon. It is not a simple matter to say where the line should be drawn between transparent and opaque, open and closed systems. Even command line Operating Systems like MS-DOS represent data as 'files', when they are 'actually' flipped bits in a stack. Flipped bits are 'really' electronic pulses. Which descriptive level we want to work on is a matter of pragmatic judgement, although as observed in chapter one, some levels are inherently more empowering and more realistic than others. The degree of choice and the underlying issues at stake, though, increase in complexity and importance as the descriptions become more metaphorical. Paradoxically, as the PC interface becomes more loaded with symbols and simulated contexts of meaning for users, it seems to consolidate systematisation.

There is, then, an ongoing politics of the interface. In certain contexts, austerity is undergoing something of a revival. The 'open source' movement, which involves the widespread sharing of programs via the Internet, perpetuates some of the ideals and ethos of the early hackers.[19] The legacy of the conflict described in the first section of this chapter, has not been the straightforward triumph of one kind of interface (the user-friendly 'desktop') over another (the text-based, black screen). In fact, people who work with machines on a daily basis naturally come to value the kind of power that more challenging systems offer them in their work. The battle of the interface has not, therefore, been lost so much as it is being re-fought in the larger world. Which kind of interface goes where is being determined locally, by the needs of money and power, but also by people in practice. The friendly interface encourages us to relate only to it, but this conflicts with our practical experience, which tells us that we need to comprehend the machine. This discrepancy represents a space within social experience. In this space, the true experience of the thing – its creation through the labouring activity of humans – comes to appear in an inverted, passive and yet controlling image of that thing. This space used to be discussed in terms of commodity fetishism, or reification. There is still scope here for a political contest over the future shape of PCs and other technological artefacts and, as just indicated, this contest is ongoing. Marcuse's vision of a new technology that might open out onto a more liberated form of social life may not be the task of an oppositional elite. It may instead fall to all of us as PC 'users'. This raises the question of which re-aestheticisations of computer technology are socially desirable.

---

[19] An interesting example of this is the 'VIM' word-processing program, which is an austere alternative to mass produced, 'off the shelf' packages like 'Word'. VIM is freely available from: www.vim.co.uk.

Chapter 3

The Aesthetics of Personal Computing

Introduction

In chapter one I suggested that technical reason, or folk technology, may have a more positive role to play in shaping contemporary society and culture than traditional critical theory has allowed. The last chapter argued that the technophiliac hacker sub-culture contributes values and a perspective on computers that may be usefully incorporated into contemporary social and cultural critique. In this chapter I will develop this line of thought in the context of a discussion of the aesthetics of personal computing. Feenberg's notion that technology is re-aestheticised as it becomes more widely employed and effectively 'codified' for social use invites discussion of which aesthetic standards and criteria in connection with the PC are most consonant with the values of critical theory. Design critique of the PC must establish how the technology should present itself to its human users, consistent with open and free communication and universal access to educational resources as guiding social principles. In this chapter I will look at the evolution of interface design standards and argue that, although they are often overtly aesthetic as well as technical, the dominant views on interface design effectively codify hegemonic interests into the social shaping of PC technology.

The core idea of this chapter, however, is that the computer itself is critical technology, in the sense that it involves its human users in the kind of reflection that drives learning and development, as well as facilitating communication. The two processes are related, since more adept technology users will find that, in the informational society, they are also the people with the resources they need to participate effectively as citizens. Knowledge and education cannot be separated from communication and participation. As suggested in chapter one, in computerised societies technical understanding is a reflexive pre-condition for either. The interface and the orientation that the PC user takes towards the machine are two sides of an experience that is at once technical and aesthetic in character. A politicised aesthetics of PC use must, therefore, address the attitude or temperament that the user brings to the machine as well as and in relation to the design of the technology. In her development of the idea of a 'computational aesthetic', Sherry Turkle develops a typology of styles of PC use. In this chapter I will attempt to build on this idea towards a theory of computational temperaments, which is partly a function of the PC interface and which becomes the basis for sociological theorisation of the game playing and hacking subject positions, which is carried out in chapters four and five respectively.

In this chapter I argue for a kind of consistency between the early hacker ideal of machine transparency and of an austere and challenging relationship with the machine and a modernist aesthetics of PC design. This forms the basis for a critical perspective on contemporary interface design and modern PC use. I begin by looking at Turkle's notion that seductive, graphical and multi-media interfaces dovetail with post-modern aesthetics. I relate this to the idea introduced at the end of the last chapter, that these interfaces extend and deepen the hold of reification, or the obfuscation through complex mediations, of the material basis of social life. On this basis, I explore some of the key concepts behind contemporary interface design looking initially at some neglected texts from the 1980s, before the graphical user interface became the design standard, and then at some more visionary notions that inform current research. This discussion highlights the sense in which the 'user friendly' interface constitutes a design hegemony within technology production, in the sense discussed in chapter one. Alternative design principles may be found in the aggressive modernist aesthetics of Bertolt Brecht, which emphasise the elimination of comfortable illusions in pursuit of truth, as the necessary condition of freedom. I suggest that this aesthetic persists, informing the daily practice of PC users. The latter oscillate between an aesthetic of passive acceptance of interface illusions and one of motivated experimentation and exploration. Movement between these two action orientations is the basis of life in computerised societies and it constantly subverts the hegemonic interface.

The PC now legitimately occupies almost every conceivable kind of social space. It mediates much social interaction, stretching our understanding of the spatial and temporal limits on the latter, and it inserts a whole new layer of behavioural complexity into our physical environment. As Nicholas Negroponte has put it, 'Computing is not about computers any more. It is about living.' (Negroponte 1995: 6). Discussion of personal computing and PC technology can no longer be limited to 'technology studies', or the study of 'human-computer interaction'. Reflection on how people behave in connection with computers and on how computers are designed to occupy social space has the potential to *be* critical social and cultural analysis. The PC has impacted on the quality of lived experience and has affected our ability to reflect on and make judgements about it. It also offers new ways to think about and to shape the experience of the future. In the context of this appraisal of the cultural significance of the PC – its aesthetic dimension – this chapter argues that modernist aesthetic values and principles provide a resource with which to explore and change the human cultural response to technological change.

Modernism/Post-modernism at the PC Interface

Sherry Turkle is right to maintain that, 'the traditional distance between people and machines has become harder to maintain' (1996: 21) – the PC is transgressive technology. Originally, this was because the PC hovered on the boundary between life and inert matter; intelligence and stupidity; thought and mere law-governed behaviour. This made the computer fascinating. Now, though, this fascination, '…once tied to the seductions of programming, …is tied to the seductions of the interface' (1996: 31). On this account, what was once an encounter between a machine on one side and a human being assuming the attitude of technical experimentation on the other, has been transformed into something we are used to thinking of as opposite to this. Computers have become aesthetic objects and how we approach them is a matter of taste.

Turkle had already pioneered the notion of a 'computational aesthetics' in her *The Second Self: Computers and the Human Spirit* (1984). In the early 1980s, computers presented their users with black screens and 'command lines', which were often green. To get the machine to do anything it was necessary to master some knowledge of computer systems architecture, data structures and programming syntax. Turkle studied people playing and working with these computers and developed a typology of 'computational styles' based on her observations. She describes a number of reactions to the austere PC interface. 'Hackers', for example, were distinguished from 'hobbyists'. The former enjoyed experimenting with new bits of code to see what novel effects they could generate while minimising strain on the computer's resources. Hobbyists revelled in the psychological security of knowing every aspect of the inner workings of their machines. These computational styles translated into very different attitudes towards programming and interacting with PCs, which Turkle correlated to gender psychology, with male 'hackers' enjoying a 'top down mastery' derived from adherence to known rules, while female enthusiasts preferred a more flexible approach that involved trial and error with code. This diversity of styles constituted the computational aesthetics of the demanding yet open interfaces of the first mass-marketed PCs.

However, from the mid-1980s, with the rise of the Apple Mac and then Windows as industry standard,

> …personal computers began to present themselves as opposed and even hostile to the traditional modernist expectation that one could take a technology, open the hood and see inside …it made the computer screen a world unto itself. It encouraged play and tinkering. Master[y]… meant getting the lay of the land rather than finding out the hierarchy of the underlying structure and rules. (1996: 35)

The new emphasis on play, surface manipulation and action in a context comprised entirely out of symbols that are irreducible to any physical referent (1996: 47) aligns the new PC interfaces with post-modern cultural theory. In fact, Turkle argues that, 'computers embody post-modern theory and bring it down to earth' (1996: 18). She contrasts this with modernist aesthetics, which she deliberately aligns with the 'elitist' culture around personal computing before the rise of the graphical interface: 'The modernist view of reality is characterised by such terms as 'linear', 'logical', 'hierarchical', and by having 'depths' that can be plumbed and understood' (1996: 17). This was the perspective of the hacker 'priesthood', who, as seen in chapter two, were defeated in the battle for control of the computer interface. PCs, Turkle argues, are no longer consistent with this attitude. They are flexible, negotiable and incorporate levels and degrees of ambiguity normally associated with aesthetic works, rather than technological artefacts. Writing in a similar vein, Richard Coyne argues that, 'It is ironic that one of twentieth century rationalism's driving metaphors, information technology, now seems to seriously challenge the fundamentals of rationalism.' (Coyne 1995: 102)

The idea that the graphical PC interface introduces something quite new into our experience of the world underpins Turkle's assertion that, 'we are moving from a modernist culture of calculation to a postmodernist culture of simulation' (1996: 20). The PC no longer presents to us as a challenging tool. It has become a source of representations and experiences that are pleasurable or stimulating in themselves, which we can enjoy without ever thinking that we are using technology. However, there is nothing in these reflections on the transgressive character of the PC interface that is specific to postmodernism as a cultural context.[1] Modernist art already calls into question the notion that art is purely representative (a medium) while technology is instrumental. For modern artists and composers, the implication of technique and the reality of technical manipulation as an integral part of the creation of the aesthetic, explains the self-reflexivity that is evident in modernist painting, poetry and music. As one historian of modernism writes:

> Modernist work is allowed to incorporate ambiguity and contradiction – in the conflict and complex implications of unresolved discord, the impossible materialisation of space, the apocalyptic tensions between colour and shapes with an emotional charge, and the oscillation between brush stroke as an object in itself and as representation of something other, these contradictions deny the transparency of the medium. They inevitably draw our attention to the language of the work, which the artist may be tempted to make more and more 'about' its own procedures. (Butler 1994: 76)

From a modernist viewpoint, the form and function of the interface are inseparably interconnected. The novelty of the PC seems to lie in the fact that it starts out as technology and becomes more aesthetic, but in doing so it converges with modernist tendencies in the aesthetic sphere, which steer art towards greater self-awareness of its technical side.

If Turkle is wrong to suggest that there is anything peculiarly post-modern about the experience of using a PC, she is surely correct to grasp the process in terms of a 'computational aesthetics'. The appeal of this notion lies in its grasp of the role of human agency in shaping the meaning and structure of activity in connection with an object. As emphasised in chapter one, technology does not determine the shape or significance of human endeavour. Rather, human cultural patterns identify some objects as technological and this identification entails an experimental attitude towards them; one which assumes that they have a relation to

---

[1] A point made repeatedly in connection with similar claims for other cultural phenomena by Alex Callinicos in his *Against Postmodernism* (1989).

human purposes such that they may usefully amplify action upon the world. What distinguishes the PC is not that it escapes identification as technology, nor that it resists this minimal technological orientation. Rather, it is uniquely 'open' technology, in the sense that it remains unclear just what the PC is actually 'for' in many contexts where people encounter it. The most ordinary PC use retains something of the character of an experiment. At the same time, the modern PC interface tends to be designed in ways that reflect a conscious desire to close off this openness and inhibit the basic technological orientation, by steering human beings into 'obvious' uses of the machine. While the interface might seem like the kind of 're-aestheticisation' envisaged by Feenberg in his theory of secondary instrumentalisation, I prefer to interpret it as a pseudo-aestheticisation, for reasons that will become clearer below. Those who challenge contemporary design standards generally do so by discovering the machine within. In this way, they, often without realizing it, re-activate the aesthetics of the modernist *avant garde*, which advocated unity of form and content – the integration of practical realism and taste.

The Hegemonic Interface

A definitive account of the function of the PC interface is provided by Donald Norman (Draper and Norman 1986). Successful interface design consists in getting the right fit between the designer's conception of the computer system and the user's 'conceptual model'. The first understands the digital-logical character of the machine and its ordering into layers and modular components – memory, processor, drives etc. – and concatenates these into a determinate machine with built-in functions. The second contains a discrete notion of what some person wants to do; a disposition to act described in terms of a practical purpose or end in mind. The task of the interface is to get the computer to represent itself to its putative users in such a way that the gulf between these two 'conceptual models' is bridged. The interface presents what Norman calls a 'System Image', through which the machine represents itself to its human user in such a way as to shape their understanding of their own best course of action so that it is consistent with successful use of the computer. A viable user model, therefore, 'results from the way the user interprets the System Image' (Draper and Norman 1986: 47).

The interface should also bridge what Norman calls the 'gulf of execution' and the 'gulf of evaluation'. The first concerns the necessity of being able to see at any given time that your actions as a computer user pertain to something you are trying to achieve, so that they retain some meaning for you as your actions. The second involves the need for feedback from the machine that supports the association of the user's ideas about what they are doing and the machine's operations. These two gulfs can be consistently bridged either by designing systems that match the inputs they need and the outputs they generate to the flow of psychological states experienced by users,[2] or by moving 'the normal descriptions of the goals and intentions closer to the description required by the physical system' (Draper and Norman 1986: 39). It is useful to think of Norman's as the minimal, or neutral specifications for interface design. Any interface must relate the computer to the user's concerns and retain their interest while their concerns are being addressed. The notion of a 'system image' grasps this well, without prejudging any matters of significance. An interface that did not project some kind of system image, that is, represent the machine in some way to human beings, would not be an 'interface'. As a minimal specification this leaves the detail of the human-machine encounter, such as the cognitive burdens placed on the user as a condition of effective use or the aesthetics of the way the machine is presented untouched. These questions are *political* and, as such, inherently contentious rather than technologically determined, or, as much of the human-computer interaction (H-CI) literature would have it, settled with reference to supposedly universal norms of cognitive psychology. As Nielsen puts it, 'The overall accessibility of a computer system is a function of its social acceptability and its practical accessibility' (1995: 280).

Superficially, the dominant emphasis on 'ease of use' and 'usability' over more technical design models represents a victory for non-technical people whom, we are told, are now able to experience the joys of computing without having to master anything technical. However, the modernist principle of self-reflexivity challenges this idea. In drawing attention to the stuff of the painting, for example, modern art refuses to separate itself off from questions of technique and of practical involvement in the world. It acknowledges its status as a product or outcome of vulgar processes and refuses the option of giving the viewer a comfortable, or 'pseudo-natural' experience. Eugene Lunn describes this in the following way:

> Modern artists, writers, and composers often draw attention to the media or materials with which they are working, the very processes of creation in their own craft. (Lunn 1986: 34)

The point of such an approach is to refuse comfortable, or seductive illusions in favour of an art that is more honest and more likely to enlighten its audience about the true character of what is being represented. This option remains open to interface designers. The transgressive character of PC technology, as described by Turkle, is not in doubt, but how we choose to explore this and to what ends is an open question. At issue between modernist and postmodernist understandings is not the association of the former with an outmoded way of thinking, or an old

---

[2] The association of memorability with meaningfulness is a standard protocol of interface design. See, for example, Preece *et al* (1994: 109); Dix *et al* (1993: 370-3), and Schneidermann's eighth 'golden rule of interface design', which is to reduce the short-term memory load of the user (1997: 75).

technology, but questions of a political, ethical and aesthetic character.[3] The implication of technique and pleasure is not original to postmodernism.

Contemporary interface design involves organising a set of pre-packaged functions around a central metaphor. The most well known example of this is the 'Windows' system, where a series of frames allows the user to view discrete clusters of icons each of which denotes a particular program. This graphical organisation of screen space, perhaps incorporating sounds, is supposed to facilitate the ready accessibility discussed above. Turkle argues that graphical interfaces possess a 'natural pluralism' (1996: 33), whereby users can come to them with diverse styles and be equally successful. Turkle suggests that interaction with a PC resembles 'human' contexts of action more than it does traditional technical ones:

> The new opaque interfaces... represented more than a technical change. These new interfaces modelled a way of understanding that depended on getting to know a computer through interacting with it, as one might get to know a person or explore a town. (1996: 23)

This, however, reifies these contexts of action – getting to know a person, or wandering around a town – as involving ways of orientating one's self to the world that are somehow 'more natural', or 'human' than when we approach technology, as if technical attitudes had no role to play in them. At the same time, it implicitly denies that the orientation to understand or explore can be part of our orientation to technical processes. This fetishism of the 'non-technical' is a betrayal of Turkle's commitment, described in the previous section, to the computer as transgressive of the distinction between art and science, the human and the technical. There is a practical, instrumental dimension to all human action and none is free from aesthetic significance if we choose to view it in that way.

A second reification follows closely on this one, namely, the reification of the system image as something that simulates this 'non-technical' context of action. Having first mistaken some action contexts as 'human', 'natural' and 'non-technical', interfaces are designed to simulate these for the human user. The effects of this double reification are clear in much contemporary interface theory. Hence, Steven Johnson writes that 'the interface is an autonomous entity' (1995: 50), suggesting that, in attaining the status of a 'work of culture' it necessarily escapes any technical determination. Turkle herself emphasises that the world at the interface constitutes a new cultural space which, 'is not reducible to lines of code, bits of data, or digital signals' (1996: 42) and stresses the independence of this new realm from 'simple physical referents' (1996: 47). Brenda Laurel bases her interpretation of interface aesthetics on an extended analogy with the theatre and argues that the user '...should be engaged, pleased or even delighted by the experience...' (Laurel 1993: 48), while the mechanics that make it possible must be withheld at all costs. In these interpretations of the interface, its 'aesthetic'

---

[3] An argument for the continued relevance of modernist cultural values under contemporary social conditions is made forcibly by Jurgen Habermas (1985: 336-367).

potential obscures its technical function entirely; it is as if the interface has converted the machine into a 'purely' artistic medium.

These descriptions reify the computer, exaggerating its power as a force independent of the knowledge and expertise of its human user. Modern computers are powerful, but only when human beings are able to use them in an intelligent way. Writing in the mid-1970s, and perhaps anticipating the rise of the artificially intelligent interface, R.S. Nickerson argued that responsible design of interactive systems should 'make the system appear to be exactly as intelligent as, or at least no more intelligent than, it really is' (Nickerson 1976: 108). This principle, including its ethical dimension, is largely overlooked in contemporary interface design. Instead, the potential of humans armed with computers is mis-represented as the power of computers to take on the core functions of humans. Paradoxically, by projecting a system image of the machine as an all-powerful source of 'easy' simulations, the interface actually reduces the power of the machine in direct proportion as it inhibits the user from having to think about what s/he is doing. While the interface seems to be a 're-aestheticisation' of the technical, in Feenberg's terms, it is actually the product of a hegemony whose central aim is to stymie the technology on one side and to thwart the technical orientation of human actors on the other. In short, the interface is produced in accordance with a design hegemony, which distorts the natural development of technology in defence of the dominant social and economic forces in informational capitalism.

This is not to suggest that there is a deliberate conspiracy within interface design and the discipline of human-computer interaction. Much of this literature is concerned with benign objectives that consciously prioritise the interests of workers and end-users. However, the dominant paradigm within the field now reflects the concern to steer computer users away from discovering things for themselves by experimenting with machines. While this may be intended to help people achieve their objectives more easily – a benign objective – it also presupposes a model of technical development according to which designers know in advance what those objectives are. Interfaces codify some actions on a PC as legitimate and conceal other possibilities by rendering them unthinkable for the ordinary user. The controlling hand that steers the user is to be dressed in the comforting woollen mitten of the 'friendly' interface. This is the underlying logic that motivates the design of self-consciously aesthetic interfaces. A good illustration is Brenda Laurel's call for interfaces modelled on theatre.

Aesthetics and Power

Laurel argues that interface designs resemble theatrical productions: 'Both theatrical design and graphical interface design are aimed at creating representations of *worlds that are like reality only different*' (Laurel 1993: 10). Her main innovation is to use Aristotelian categories to construct a theory of how the interface ought to project a system image that embodies naturalistic theories of drama. Just as with theatre, the objective of good interface design is to steer the user through a series of events without their ever sensing that they are being steered. The sequence of events flows 'naturally', from the introduction of characters through to the revelation of their true purpose, which is disclosed by the drama as a whole. Laurel argues that both theatre and interface design are species of dramaturgy and that, 'The orchestration of probability and causality is the stuff that dramaturgy is made of' (Laurel 1993: 81). Successful interface design depends upon successfully constructing a system of implicit constraints, so that explicit constraints are never needed. Laurel candidly states that for the user of her ideal system, '...the technical magic that supports the representation, as in the theatre, is behind the scenes, ...the representation is all there is...' (Laurel 1993: 17).

This is exactly the kind of pseudo-naturalism that Bertolt Brecht attacked in his development of a Marxist-modernist theatre. Brecht argued that when producing art or cultural objects for a mass public, or 'popular art', we must 'keep the fact of deception in sight' (Bloch *et al* 1979: 81). Art has been used ideologically, to suppress the truth, but it can also be used to tell the truth in ways that help people to gain real empowerment – collective, shared control over the future direction of their society:

> In the theatre, reality can be represented both in objective and in imaginative forms. The actors may not use make-up – or hardly any – and claim to be 'absolutely natural' and yet the whole thing can be a swindle; and they can wear masks of a grotesque kind and present the truth. It is hardly open to debate that the means must be questioned about the ends they serve. (In Bloch *et al* 1979: 83)

Brecht's point is that true realism, the realism of modernist aesthetics, is concerned to take apart reality as it is presented to us – it is suspicious of the obvious and natural route through any system.

An attitude of suspicion is peculiarly appropriate to the contemporary PC interface. As Sean Cubitt argues, user friendly interfaces are, in this sense, 'culturally imperialist' because they are based on a 'hyper-individualised' notion of the user (2000: 34). Computers, he writes, have been made 'in the image of an ideally isolated individual' and in line with a 'narrow visual culture' (2000: 35). Moreover,

> The success of the MAC's desktop metaphor has little to do with the mixed metaphors of windows, folders and disks and much more to do with the way their interrelation forms a grammar, a syntagmatic organisation of word processing and data management internalised as familiar. (Cubitt 2000: 4)

Icons arranged on a static background impose a narrow reading on our interaction with a computer – at any given time the actual range of possibilities open to us is much broader, while the range of options beyond each icon is also wider than the icons themselves suggest. Each icon is neatly delimited in space, occupying a discrete part of the screen. Where it is located on the screen does not affect its function. Normally, it will have a text label and will have the form of a pictorial image associated with the function it activates. There is no radical openness to interpretation here; Windows and icons impose a homogeneous order on the machine behind the 'wallpaper'.

A modernist alternative might be inspired by the principle of simultaneity. Lunn defines this as follows:

> Instead of a traditional art of transitions from one event, one sensation, one thing at a time, presented sequentially, modern art is often without apparent causal progression and completion. It is intended to exist within a open-ended and 'continuous present' in which various experiences, past and present, inner and outer, of different persons are juxtaposed, their distances eclipsed as though on a flat surface. (Lunn 1986: 35)

As the Italian futurist, Umberto Boccioni describes it, this principle involves an opening out of representation beyond the bounds of conventional logic:

> In painting a person on a balcony, seen from inside the room, we do not limit the scene to what the frame of the window renders visible; but we try to render the sum total of visual sensations which the person on the balcony has experienced; the sunbathed throng in the street, the double row of houses which stretch to right and left, the beflowered balconies etc, This implies the simultaneousness of the ambient, and, therefore, the dislocation and dismemberment of objects the scattering and fusion of details, freed from accepted logic, and independent from one another. (Cited in Butler 1994: 148)

A good illustration of the principle is provided in modernist works that, like contemporary interfaces, use the 'window' metaphor to open up viewers to new ways of experiencing meaning. Sonia Delaunay's painting 'fenêtres simultanées' consists of bands of colour, which, unlike the metaphor structure of graphical user interfaces, 'refuse any dominant light source, and so decentralise structure into an abstract pattern...' (Butler 1994: 164). The bands of colour serve to 'key' – like clefs in musical notation – the words of Robert Delaunay's poem, 'la prose transsiberien'. The meaning of each is spatially related to the other and the viewer/reader can approach the work in any number of ways. There is no 'obvious' way to read the poem, but our experience of it can be shaped by the bands of colour. Similarly, the painting can be understood differently, depending on which line of the poem (if any) we take as our starting point.

At present, hegemonic interfaces do break with the Gutenberg model of words resting passive and linear on a page, but they do not work on the critical level of, 'ask[ing] how the spatial arrangement of a series of messages might affect their meaning' (Butler 1994: 171). The icon stands in for this, precluding experimentation and exploration informed by a range of intersecting message forms (colour, spatial ordering, semantics, semiotics). Such configurations at the interface seem to be exactly what one of the pioneers of personal computing, Ted Nelson has in mind, though, when he describes his alternative to metaphor as the organising principle of interface design. He likens the functional elements in a system to a bunch of coins in your hand:

If you think about all the things you want a design to do, and at first they don't fit together, the thing to do is *jingle them in your mind* until they stack up together. The result will be some gradual organisation of these desiderata into a usable set of principles, aligning in some new fashion. (Nelson 1990: 240)

In contrast to this kind of approach, in current design, 'slavish adherence to metaphor prevents the emergence of *things that are genuinely new*' (Nelson 1990: 239). In other words, by attempting to steer the user through a 'non-technical' interaction with a technological artefact contemporary interface design limits itself to developing poor simulations of something that has never existed ('purely' aesthetic experience, free of the taint of technology). Indeed, most often the ideal of an aestheticised interface is effectively betrayed by a segregation of the functional and the artistic, with the latter assigned to predetermined status as 'screensavers', or 'wallpaper', rather than integrated into the delivery of functionality proper.

The idea of simultaneity is central to Lev Manovich's conception of the computer as a 'new medium' that is transforming contemporary culture. Manovich (2001) observes that many 'digital artists' fail to probe the technical limits of their modern machine, although he fails to identify the interface as an inhibiting factor that might explain this. Even despite this, however, he argues that the logic of the computer as a digital storage medium entails a shift in the nature of contemporary aesthetic experience. Whereas film and other pre-digital media organised representations sequentially, so that we experienced them as the passage of time, computers revive an experience, which he calls 'pre-modern', of spatial montage in which different representations co-exist simultaneously in our experience. Manovich illustrates this with reference to frames and windows, but he traces it to the underlying architecture of the computer, which is essentially defined as a database plus algorithms. In his vision, computers are naturalising elements of radical modernism by installing principles of collage (cut and paste), non-photographic realism and the spatialisation of experience into patterns of daily life. Viewed in this way, his own new media theory represents an attempt to theorise the computer on its own terms, whereas interface theory is concerned to superimpose established models of human experience as metaphors that order and contain user behaviour.

Privileged Perspectives

It is as the harbinger of a culturally ubiquitous 'simulation aesthetic' that Turkle claims the interface embodies post-modern theory and brings it down to earth. It is difficult to tell if she enjoys the irony in her own formulation. Her point is that graphical interfaces provide us with a level of discourse around computers that subverts the authority of electrical engineering or programming. These are not authoritative narratives on the computer, but merely alternative ways of discussing a computer and of acting in connection with it. Equally valid, in an epistemological sense, is the user's attitude: 'A user is involved with the machine in a hands-on way, but is not interested in the technology except as it enables an application' (1996: 32). The user knows how to operate the graphical interface and, therefore, how to achieve the things s/he wants to with the machine. Users are unlikely to know anything about the machine behind the interface, but they do not need to know anything about that because their purposes in using the computer are not related to computing. This comports well with a post-modernist thesis on culture more generally because it suggests the absence of privileged perspectives on reality, or grand narratives that disclose more of the truth than other, more trivial ones. Post-modernism rejects the notion that some truths are 'deeper' or more profound than others. As Turkle puts it: 'In the culture of simulation, if it works for you it has all the reality it needs' (Turkle 1996: 24).

Graphical environments give the user '...a scintillating surface on which to float, skim and play', where there is 'nowhere left to dive' (1996: 34). The new interfaces have, 'introduced a way of thinking that put a premium on surface manipulation and working in ignorance of the underlying mechanism' (1996: 35). As Baudrillard argues in his seminal essay on the culture of simulation, these programmed worlds are experienced by people as if they were real, or even 'more real than reality' (Baudrillard 1994: 34). Hanging on to a more realistic perspective, Steven Johnson notes that the graphical interface introduced a paradox into the experience of using a computer:

> There was a strangely paradoxical quality to direct manipulation: in reality, the graphic interface had added another layer separating the user from his or her information. But the tactile immediacy of the illusion made it seem as though the information was now closer at hand, rather than farther away. (Johnson 1995: 21)

According to Turkle, the paradox is only apparent if we hang on to the idea, which after all is only a metaphor, of more fundamental layers within the machine. She insists:

> The objects on the screen have no simple physical referents. In this sense, life on the screen is without origin and foundation. It is a place where signs taken for reality may substitute for the real. Its aesthetic has to do with manipulation and recombination. (Turkle 1996: 47)

Richard Coyne also argues that,

> ...the entire computer system is imbued with metaphor, from the structure and configuration of hardware to icons and the designation of object-like names attached to program subroutines. (Coyne 1995: 250)

In his view, '...metaphor practically permeates our entire conception of the computer' (Coyne 1995: 253). The fact that we are always using metaphors when we speak and think about the computer suggests that there is no epistemologically privileged vantage point on it. Any true remark a user can make about the behaviour of an interface is as true as any true statement a programmer makes about the architecture of a program. And the importance of each will depend on who you are in relation to the computer and what you are hoping to do with it. No point of view is eminently more sensible, revealing, or useful than any other.

As seen in chapter one, it is reasonable to argue that there is no sense to be made of a computer or any other technical artefact outside of the social conditions that constitute it as a determinate object of experience. It seems to follow from this that any given verbal construction, so long as it is accurate, is as good as any other. In fact, though, even if we work with a variety of levels of description of any given thing in the course of our dealings with it, common sense urges us to accept that there is a physical description, or way of talking about that thing which has a kind of priority. If we find ourselves talking about a thing that has no tangible, physical presence then we are apt to question the sense of our own activities. This is not to deny that people do this. Commonly, we are thrown in the social practice of talking about lots of things that do not have a physical or manifest presence. This is because social interaction and culture generate vast amounts of short-hand expressions that allow us to express meaning to each other, although when subjected to philosophical scrutiny, their literal meanings are obscure. Metaphor may be ubiquitous in our experience, including our experience of computers but, as Davidson (1980) has argued, it has its origins in literal speech about the world. Some layers of discourse are more fundamental than others, even though the latter class are for practical reasons ineliminable and irreducible to the former. The obvious example is that of mind – we talk about our ideas, thoughts and feelings all the time, but we know that the descriptions we use supervene on those of neuro-physical states. Brain chemistry could, in principle, provide me with a more comprehensive set of explanations for my moods but this does not lead me to want to give up contemplating them in a poetic way, because the supervening kind of description ties in with my practical needs as a feeling creature in a culture which sets some kind of value on introspection.

A similar argument applies to the computer. We know that descriptions of the computer that disclose its architecture as a technological system and the programming regulating its behaviour at any given time contain more comprehensive information about it than, for example, my frustrated observation that the 'back' button seems not be working. The point of this argument is not to assert a dogmatic physicalism about computers, which would be naïve in view of the ontological character of software. Rather, I want to suggest that some levels are more profound because of the way that they mesh with the structures of human action in relation to computers and, in particular, because they correspond to different degrees of user empowerment. Quine says somewhere that it is not their more physical character that makes us sure that molecules exist, it is the fact that we have been talking and thinking about them for so long that they have acquired a kind of certainty not shared by more recent entrants into our ontology. As the computer becomes fixed in our evolutionary history we will find that some parts of it are the technical reality – they are the technical elements that always have to be present when there is a computer. Necessarily, they correspond to that which is most physically recalcitrant in the structure of the machine and to the socially and culturally mediated decisions concerning what the machine is to be used for.

In this context, Manovich's suggestion that the database-algorithm structure of the computer is culturally determinate is more realistic than Turkle and Coyne's focus on its role as a vehicle for simulation and metaphor. Arguing that, 'To understand the logic of new media, we need to turn to computer science' (2001: 48), Manovich identifies the culturally salient properties of the computer as follows:

> If in physics the world is made of atoms and in genetics it is made of genes, computer programming encapsulates the world according to its own logic. The world is reduced to two kinds of software objects that are complementary to each other – data structures and algorithms. Any process or task is reduced to an algorithm, a final sequence of simple operations that a computer can execute to accomplish a given task. And any object in the world – be it the population of a city, or the weather over the course of a century, or a chair, or a human brain – is modelled as a data structure, that is, data organised in a particular way for search and retrieval. Examples of data structures are arrays, linked lists, and graphs. Algorithms and data structures have a symbiotic relationship. The more complex the data structure of a computer program, the simpler the algorithm needs to be, and vice versa. Together, data structures and algorithms are two halves of the ontology of the world according to a computer. (2001: 223)

The database/algorithm structure is essential to all computer systems architecture and is fundamental to the logical operation of all computers, dating back at least to Turing and probably even to Babbage. If there is an essential definition of a 'computer' then it is something that performs a series of logical operations on a set of data.

This discussion also highlights the importance of drawing on Feenberg's critical social constructionism when assessing the evolution of the computer as technological medium. As noted above, Manovich neglects the social factors, in particular those condensed in the interface itself, that inhibit the development of free cultures of use and experimentation with the new medium.[4] In his assessment of computers as 'new media', a (subtle) technical determinism creeps into his position at key points. Although he says that, 'to develop a new aesthetics of new media, we should pay as much attention to cultural history as to the computer's unique new possibilities to generate, organise, manipulate and distribute data' (2001: 314), this is not always what he does. For example, he explains the development of contemporary interface design principles essentially by citing the causal influence of film, which he considers the dominant medium of the Twentieth Century. Digitisation then reacts back upon cinema, producing the reintegration of spatial montage and animation to the mainstream of cinematic culture. These are useful insights, but they neglect the role of human beings

---

[4] Manovich acknowledges that the interface has a kind of autonomy, pointing out that, '...far from being a transparent window into the data inside a computer, the interface brings with it strong messages of its own' (2001: 65).

making choices that mediate between media, which are instead presented as influencing each other behind the backs of their human users. The cinematic influence on interface design is part of a collection of cultural influences that reflect the hold of specific social forces on hegemonic technology design standards.[5] Similarly, the way in which the digital reacts back on cinema needs to be understood in terms of broader cultural tendencies that promote a kind of attenuated realism: *non*-digital movies like *Amélie*; magic realism in literature, and the much-discussed 'infantilisation' of culture generally must all be factors here.

These factors might seem to do little more than complement Manovich's brilliant analysis of *media*. But I believe his neglect of the broader dimension leads him to write as if his own vision of an educated computer using population using their PCs in an experimental way to express themselves artistically faced little or no resistance from social forces who are, at best, uninterested in the creative potential of ordinary people. As we have seen, the design of the PC interface is a significant constraining measure, inhibiting free creativity and experimentation. This reflects prior design hegemonies and embodies social interests that work to shape technological media and their patterns of mutual interpenetration. Consequently, while Manovich correctly identifies many of the radical possibilities of new media and traces the exploitation of these to the need for technical competencies he fails to see that exploiting these will be transgressive of, and not in conformity with, dominant tendencies in interface design. It may even take us into conflict with key players in the economy and society at large. Manovich's position amounts to a kind of passivity in cultural politics, something which is most clear when he discusses Benjamin's suggestion that the capitalism of his time was training people in the use of their senses, to make them thoroughly compliant to the needs of the system. Having reviewed Benjamin's position on the training of our human sensorium by capitalism, Manovich writes:

> If Benjamin appears to regret that the subjects of industrial society lost their pre-modern freedom of perception, now regimented by the factory, the modern city and film, we may instead think of the information density of our own workspaces as a new aesthetic challenge, something to explore rather than condemn. (2001: 330)

---

[5] Manovich maintains, for example, that increased use of 3-D spatial representations in new media objects is 'inevitable' (2001: 214) because it corresponds to the underlying structure of the computer's world and because this is consistent with the influence of film, which is culturally dominant. But, as indicated in chapter two, the idea of using the computer to project a visually compelling fictional world was the outcome of political choices. Blind and visually impaired computer users were excluded from the computer culture as a result of this decision (See Goggin and Newell 2003). Moreover, as the computer game 'Broken Sword 3' illustrates, the move to 3-D can be a reflection of the influence of fashion rather than related to any actual improvements in the quality of new media products. From the point of view of the player, the game is essentially unchanged by the new 'spatial' dimension, suggesting that the reasons for its inclusion are social – the need to be up-to-date and make a saleable commodity – rather than a drive to exploit the technology for superior aesthetic effects. I am grateful to Elia 'Toops' Tupou for bringing this example to my attention.

In fact, in the computer age we should be more suspicious of the implicit constraints that steer us without our knowing it. And we should be suspicious of our own motivations for entering a realm whose basic architecture we do not comprehend, even though it is not natural but of 'our' making. As seen in the previous section, the graphical user interface is organised in accordance with a sovereign, authorial narrative that guides the human user through the technologically supported 'reality'. To go along with it is to cynically accept its 'guidance' and authority, even though we know that what it is telling us is a convenient fiction (you have 'filed' that document), which will shortly break down, and that recognition of the technical – with its real constraints – is always an option and, at some point, inevitable. In this way, the graphical user interface actually introduces a binary opposition, or straight choice for users, in place of openness: conform or hack. From a modernist perspective, it is the homogenising voice of the interface as a system of implicit constraints that should be suspect:

> Instead of an omniscient and reliable narrator, modern writers develop either single or multiple, but all limited and fallible, vantages from which to view events. (Lunn 1986: 36)

In its place we should insist on interfaces that are genuinely open, in the sense that they hold open a diversity of perspectives on the underlying machine, should we want to use them, and allow us to interfere with the behaviour of the technology at whatever levels we choose.

In this context, it is interesting that Ted Nelson likens his ideal interface as one that presents the system as a 'globe':

> A globe is my model of a proper information system. A globe does not say 'good morning'; it does not bother you with menus, icons, or prompts. You turn it or move your head to the most useful position for overview or detail, that's all. These crypto-social models have created a false trail of design directions, and are wasting effort and misdirecting hopes. (Nelson 1990: 237)

Such openness is only valuable, though, if is acknowledged that the deeper one goes into a system, the more 'open' it is to understanding and control. As seen already, Turkle's post-modernism leads her to reject the idea that some perspectives are intrinsically privileged over others. Here, Turkle attempts to revive her sense of transgression, arguing that programming itself has become a more flexible operation resembling 'cutting and pasting – albeit at a high level of abstraction', within which a number of different styles can be seen emerging (with the inevitable consequence that more women are doing it than ever before). There is then, no systematic qualitative difference between programming and working at a more superficial level of the machine. Neither is more profound than the other and the control they afford is ultimately the same. This is, however, an exaggeration. It is true that, as the number of layers in the PC system increases so there are more 'pseudo-technical' ones opening up in the middle. Most programmers will argue strongly that HTML is not a programming language, though, because it lacks the requisite difficulty and does not require you to think in terms of the underlying data structures that support your effects. Turkle is simply wrong to suggest that a more flexible style of human computer interaction is now emerging even at these levels, because you can't 'negotiate' with a compiler and the hard logic is binary in its consequences: your program either works or it doesn't. The scope for transgression here is not provided by changes in the nature of the technology, but by the social context of computing.

Although she argues that there has been a proliferation of computational styles, Turkle has done more than most to clarify the sociological fact that we are increasingly confronted with two, opposed possibilities: 'Hackers are the antithesis of users. They are passionately involved in mastery of the machine itself' (1996: 32). This binary opposition is itself a consequence of the interface that forces us to choose between physical resignation and compliance, or the kind of re-embodiment that comes from deciding to hack the interface. Interestingly, Manovich also distinguishes between the 'Data dandy', who surfs the Net collecting data, and the web 'explorer', who is drawn more to the experience of traversing virtual space, including game spaces (Manovich 2001: 271). These observations disclose the sociological significance of Sean Cubitt's call to refuse the homogenised experience of reading that, he says, accompanies digitalisation:

> What we must require of a digital aesthetic is not negation but refusal of the condition of the universal text, a secular blasphemy against the objectification of the world, our bodies and our others. Recorporealisation will imply, against the thingness of world, body and other, their mutual interpenetration, and it will depend on the materials in which they are mediated, including, ...the mutual permeation of human and machine. (Cubitt 2000: 23-4)[6]

In the design of computers for autonomous, socially responsible users, the technical reality must be acknowledged. From the standpoint of a modernist aesthetics, this is not something to be feared, but rather an opportunity to create novel artefacts and to experiment with basic environmental structures of contemporary social life. This would be a realization of Ted Nelson's vision of computers with open interfaces, inviting us to act directly on the underlying data structures:

> Once we leave behind 'two-dimensionality' (virtual paper) and even 'three dimensionality' (virtual stacks), we step off the edge into another world, into the representation of *the true structure and interconnectedness of information*. To represent this true structure, we need to indicate multidimensional connection and multiple connections between entities. (Nelson 1990: 241)

---

[6] It is interesting to note in relation to Felix Guattari's (1989) opposition of the iconic to the diagrammatic. The former, he argues, blocks while the latter frees up the intellect to de- and re-territorialise dominant discourses, which he associates with mass media.

Designs like this presuppose, however, an audience that is capable of responding to them and playing its part in making the experience they are designed to facilitate.

Experimentation and Education

Turkle argues that, in its impact upon individuals, the PC, especially the networked PC, feeds into the cultural context of post-modernity. In particular, she maintains that usable interfaces promote an experience of play which extends to one's self and one's identity. She writes, for example, that, '...windows have become a powerful metaphor for thinking about the self as a multiple, distributed system' (1996: 14). In cyberspace the constraints of physical being are shaken off and it becomes possible, using media like e-mail, chat rooms and multi-user domains (MUDs), to present an image to others that is of our own choosing. Men can pretend to be female; players in MUDs can assume the role of 'wizards', and people can describe themselves as more physically attractive than they are to others in chat room encounters. If they are really lucky, they may even have 'net sex' with other 'players'.

The immateriality and anonymity afforded by computer generated environments in on-line encounters reinforce the post-modernist theme of identity as something plastic and endlessly revisable. Post-modern subjects do not have more 'essential' or 'deeper' layers to their personalities, but are distributed across a single, open plane. At any given time, our selves – what we experience and how we appear to others – are effects of the discursive regime that is currently in operation. All effects are equally superficial, or equally 'deep', depending on how you choose to describe yourself (the illusion of 'depth' is merely one effect among others). As already mentioned above, post-modernism tends to assign the subject a passive role in relation to technology and this traces to the fact that the discursive constitution of interface experience is, from this perspective, the determining influence upon identity when we interact with a machine. This is why Coyne emphasises that, 'The success of the personal computer interface is largely attributable to the deliberate use of particular organisational metaphors' (1995: 284). The user is 'constructed' by the technology (Turkle 1996: 46) and does not so much enter a field of 'discursive play' (Coyne 1995: 292) defined by the interface as is produced by it.

The post-modernist view of identity comports well with a consumerist culture, in which people 'buy' products to strengthen their sense of themselves. Under such circumstances, it seems to make no sense to speak of 'reification': Our human essence has not been expropriated from us, since we never had one to take. The public sign – be it an icon or a can of beans – constitutes us and provides the order that makes experience, including 'subjective' experience, possible. Clearly, if the graphical interface was as easily accessible as it seemed to be and if the experience it held out was a seamless flow of symbols producing effects in and through us without our ever having to refer to the world beyond, then the PC interface would be an engine room in the post-modern empire of the sign. However, I have indicated that this project is misconceived – an anti-realist projection with, doubtless unintended, ideological consequences. In her more critical moments, Turkle situates the graphical interface and our apparent willingness to be seduced by it in a richer problematics of the human subject:

> If one is afraid of intimacy yet afraid of being alone, even a stand-alone (not networked) computer offers an apparent solution. Interactive and reactive, the computer offers the illusion of companionship without the demands of friendship. One can be a loner yet never be alone. (1996: 30)

This observation recalls her earlier comments, discussed in the last chapter, on computer hackers, many of whom became addicted to the routine behaviours of the machine and suffered from social and psychological withdrawal as a result. Curiously, in her *The Second Self* (1984), before she was seduced by post-modernism, Turkle wrote very similar words about those hackers and expressed her concern that they represented a pathological reaction to the computer, which she called 'entrapment' (1984: 214). In the cited passage, Turkle describes the same kind of dependency on the machine – now premised upon the seductions of simulation rather than those of programming – as existing for all users and her earlier concern seems to have evaporated. However, as Cubitt observes:

> The popularity and intensity of net experience are neither self-explanatory, nor simple effects of technological determinism or media imperialism. They belong to the political erotics of the hyperindividualised electronic subject. (2000: 87)

If we have moved to a mass psychology on the edge of entrapment then we should acknowledge and address this danger in the principles of technology design. There is an alternative to seductive interfaces and it consists in fusing the technical and the aesthetic in designs that are original and, most importantly, challenging. Interfaces are conceivable that invite users to think about their machines in a variety of different ways and to gain more levels of empowerment through such thinking. We can find precedent for such interface design principles in modernist artistic production.

Modernism does not involve regress to some optimistic, pro-enlightenment fantasy in which rational, linear thinkers move inexorably towards a perfectible utopia. Rather, modernism is committed to a 'defensive humanism', in which subjectivity, although under constant threat, cannot be annihilated, 'in spite of everything' (Sypher 1962: 156). As Butler writes,

> ...the individual enters into Modernist literature as the field of conflicting forces and desires... the essential premiss is that the individual may be subject to the dissolution of an identity which attempts to contain competing mental systems. (Butler 1994: 92)

As a site of tension, inner conflict and primal needs, the subject has to *work* to sustain a sense of self. Self-hood becomes an effort, within which the kind of experimentation described by Turkle may have a place. But such experimentation and its fruits must be integrated into an overall sense of self that is more than just a random assemblage of states ready to be activated by this or that discourse. No person is a mere, 'Humean bundle of bits of past experiences but is involved in a continuous interactive process' (Butler 1994: 142). Interfaces that deprive us of the 'cognitive burden' of memory and attempt to train us – colonising our bodies through internalised, set physical responses to known and regular stimuli – effectively renounce any place for themselves in the aesthetic sphere; they become colourful tools. The modernist alternative would be to produce interfaces that are fit for active, intelligent audiences struggling to work out how they want technology to fit into their experience of the world. In responding to this, interface designers must run the same risks as modern artists and composers, namely, that of producing works that can only be understood by people with a certain level of prior understanding.

Interfaces that observe the principles discussed in the previous sections and that are as open and supportive to exploration as they are challenging and provocative are not impractical either. Like Nickerson's recommendation that the interface should not deceive, M. Fitter's suggestion that, 'as the user becomes more proficient he should be permitted to see more of the system' (Fitter 1979: 344) turns out to be a neglected *ethical* precept of good interface design. Only interfaces that encourage experimentation and intelligent, curious responses from their users are really consistent with the efflorescence of individuality trumpeted by post-modernist talk of a politics of self-hood. Only with greater knowledge of the system do differences of individual style become important. As Butler notes, the dissonance in modernist works imposed on their audiences a need for further investigation (1994: 68) and we should expect genuinely aesthetic interfaces to do the same.

It is worth emphasising that the project of a hegemonic, post-modern interface is always likely to run up against resistance from real humans operating under determinate social and cultural conditions. Even if we knew how to simulate something that has never existed, people would not be seduced by it for long. The proposition that 'we are dumbfounded by the perfection of the programming' (Baudrillard 1994: 34) in our technological environment is falsified by contemporary culture, in aesthetics at least. In so far as it secures artistic recognition, the computer does not do so in its capacity as a super-aesthetic artefact. The computer has impacted upon the sphere of culture as a machine bearing a distinctive logic and structure. Literature and painting provide examples of artists exploiting the aesthetic significance of the underlying machine. In E.L. Doctorow's (1979) novel, 'Loon Lake', for example, we find monologues in computer style 'code' – repetition of barely meaningful lines in chunks that both denote and effect some emotional function – while in the paintings of Roman Opalka, numeric series are gently inscribed on canvasses that seem at first to be just blank and colourless. Similarly, in contemporary music it is the way that computers echo the rhythmic pulse of life in networked society that is deployed, rather than their ability to synthesise the sounds of older instruments. It would be more accurate to say that, far from generating a 'simulation aesthetic' (Turkle) the dominant computer interface simulates the (abandoned) space of a pure aesthetics.

A progressive politics of interface design would centre on the need to reclaim some of the cognitive burdens of life in contemporary society. This is linked by Cubitt to a politics of re-embodiment – a theme to which I return in the next chapter. Elements within the computer culture are actively engaged in this politics, including those who highlight the role of the interface by designing alternatives. Frequently, these involve subverting hegemonic conventions by drawing attention to the way in which different interfaces may affect our experience of the same data. An excellent illustration of this principle, discussed by Manovich, involves artists working around the theme of a loved one returning from a war. This web-site offers visitors several different interfaces to the same cluster of text messages, each affording us a different experience of the same few lines.[7] This project can be read as critical of the hegemonic paradigm, in that it promotes reflection on the nature of the interface as a discrete element in computer mediated experience. Similar web-based projects by women artists target what they see as the masculinist bias in hegemonic interface design. Mary Flanagan, for example, describes her 'phage' program as a 'beneficial virus' that enables us to think about the computer in a non-hierarchical way. The virus scours the hard drive of the host machine and applies its own organisational parameters to the data. It then displays information about the contents of the drive in what she calls 'non-Cartesian 3-D space, granting random and often unknown pieces of data trajectories, lifetimes, and the power of random movement.' The point of this is that it 'allows users to shift their own subject position amid their own data', which is represented to them in the form of an artwork, which displays 'his or her computer memory as a palimpsest of life experiences rather than as simply a tool for daily use' (Flanagan 2003: 445-9).

These interventions are motivated assaults on the project of a singularising, hegemonic interface that is trying to assimilate the identity of the PC. They highlight the reality that few people, if any, are actually 'users' in the sense that is taken for granted in mainstream HC-I. Even people who are not motivated to go any further with a computer than they really have to find that the seamless drama presented for them at the interface invariably breaks down in the course of a day's work. At these points, they are obliged to break with the illusion and start to think about the machine as a complex artefact that requires them to remember things and to experiment with it in order to achieve their objectives and to find new goals to achieve in future. In other words, the hegemonic interface fails to produce us simply as deferential users, it also induces the opposite temperament, namely, that of a curiosity that no longer respects the authority of the interface. I will develop the idea that the computer culture is now structured around the co-existence of two opposed temperaments in the next two chapters.

This chapter has argued that the PC is transgressive in that it defies the simple and obvious opposition of technology to culture, being both a source of expressive

---

[7] The site can be visited at http://www.myboyfriendcamehomefromth.ewar.ru/.

and aesthetic possibilities and experiences, and a tool for the achievement of instrumentally desired objectives. In this transgression, however, it mirrors strains in modernist cultural production, which worked out of a critique of art as something separate from technology and society. It is useful and exciting to reflect upon the implications of this convergence for the aesthetic-mechanics of the PC and especially its 'system image'. Post-modern theory starts from the observation that the PC is transgressive, but then mistakes the aesthetic or cultural sphere for the human. As such, it idealises certain contexts of human action and interaction as 'natural' or prior and sets up the successful simulation of these idealisations as goals of good technology design. This results in prescriptions for interface design that would deliberately misrepresent the computer to its human user. The graphical interface is 'open' to interpretation in the sense that it is intended to be almost anything other than what it is, namely, a technical artefact. The social implications of this are almost entirely overlooked in post-modern cultural theory, which prioritises instead the necessity of easy access to consumable identities. The convergence with modernism described above, however, is suggestive of a politics of interface design that is suspicious of the dominant association of good design with ease of use and ready similarity with other, non-computing contexts. This chapter has suggested that applying modernist aesthetic concepts to interface design may open out onto an approach that is more realistic with regard to the underlying technology and the character of most peoples' experience when using a PC. This approach would also allow interface designers to be more experimental and to present novel technology in fresh and unexpected ways. Finally, a modernist aesthetics of interface design will lead to technology that comports better with a PC user population that expects and wants to be challenged, surprised and ultimately more knowledgeable as a result of using their computers.

Chapter 4

The Cynicism of the Computer Gamer

Introduction

In this chapter I will draw on Peter Sloterdijk's notion of historical temperaments to clarify the thesis of a bifurcation of human attitudes and orientations in response to the PC interface. It has been argued that the interface is a hegemonic strategy; a codification of computer technology in line with the needs of dominant social interests. As such, the interface can never impose complete closure on the experience of the PC and I have suggested that, in its current form, it is actually inconsistent with both the technological reality and the natural human attitude towards technical artefacts, which is experimental and, in some senses, inherently instrumentalist. Resistance to the interface and attempts to contest its monopolistic hold on computer mediated experience take the form of uses of PC technology that do not follow the sequential logic asserted by interface feedback. However, if the interface is a project that is doomed to fail in any case, the first mystery is that of compliance. Why would anyone simply play along with the interface, beyond the point at which it has become merely an irritating intrusion?

Identifying the role of social factors in constructing and maintaining technological projects enables us to answer this question. This chapter looks at the computer game as interface-generated illusion with enormous holding power. The power of the interface is not explicable with reference to the technology, nor to facts about individual psychology, but only by the conjunction of the two in a specific social context. This context was and remains a society marked by a distinctive historical temperament. Turkle's typology of computational styles is useful here because it enables us to identify the conflicting action orientations that shape the demand for technology and feed into the context of interface design. In this chapter, the issue is taken up again in the context of an analysis of computer games playing, as it is here that we discover the underlying historical temperament corresponding to the aesthetic of the PC 'user'.

The chapter begins with the question of the social character of play. In the first section I review some established theories of play and look briefly at an example of the some recent, ludological scholarship that has emerged in response to the emergence of the computer game. This leads into a discussion of the ideological context which absorbed the first computer games and transformed an early, probably quite aimless hack, into mass entertainment. It is in Sloterdijk's critique of the all pervasive cynicism of the 1980s that we find the origins of the computer game play temperament and its inner structure. This turns out to be the key to its social and historical significance, which is addressed in the third section. In conclusion, I argue that the computer game as a medium and the cynical temperament which is its home in contemporary culture play a fundamental role in the technical politics that contests the PC interface.

The Sociology of Play

Play can be described in terms of its qualitative, or aesthetic qualities; its role in social learning processes, and its place in relation to various functioning social systems. Each of these dimensions of sociological enquiry pulls out different aspects of the phenomenon and corresponds to various practical interests that are codified within specific branches of knowledge. The first reflects the interest of those concerned with the sociology of childhood and ethnomethodologists interested in the character of early experience as suggestive of the aesthetic norms that underpin a culture. In the second, play is described in terms of its relation to learning, by those with an interest in educational theory and developmental psychology. Play also has its functional aspect, sorting and integrating individuals into broader social structures, especially schools and, via these, the social system as a whole. The basis for integrating these ways of describing play into a single model is that all three perspectives emphasise the centrality of learning processes in the social interpretation of play. In Habermas's phrase, learning is the 'pace-maker' (1984: 120; 160) of social evolution and we can extrapolate from this to the proposition that the way a society organises its play will be highly suggestive of its evolutionary position. The sketch developed here stresses the role of play in social learning under each of the three aspects: the subjective aesthetics of play; the acquisition of cognitive and communicative competences through play, and play as a mechanism for social integration.

Through play children gain a feel for the qualitative character of the social world they will inhabit. At this level of description, emphasis is placed on the way the world feels and the processes whereby playful activity acquaints young people with the texture of life in their society. In play we encounter a range of sensations associated with the physical world, other people, and the rules of the games played. Each of these has, to some degree, a 'world disclosing' role for us. Hence, in working class communities children play football and this introduces them to the sensation of their own physical strength as a variable in social life. Control of a heavy leather ball and the power to kick it long distances; physical contact with others, and a context that is clearly and straightforwardly regulated are all experienced by children from an early age. Through such media we are prepared for the aesthetics of our social world and learn to experience them as our own.

Learning rules for play is only one of the cognitive competencies that we associate with play. A series of lessons may be peeled away from the experiences of combining with others, winning and losing, even inventing new games, and each of these is then folded into experience away from the game playing situation. Play is of enormous significance in the developmental psychological processes whereby individuals acquire the moral capabilities of judging situations, others and themselves in later life. In play, we learn to follow rules, acquire the values associated with co-operation and fair competition, and of solidarity that transcends the game and makes playful encounters possible in the first place.[1] These lessons are essential to the development of all well-adjusted individuals and are generally extracted from the process of play and consolidated in other social settings. Children progress to more complex and demanding games, including games they invent themselves, only when they have mastered these principles and begun to apply them in other contexts.

Viewed in the round, play has the function of transmitting skills and personal qualities that are functional for social life. The institution of play itself can also be viewed as a differentiation of human activity that has evolutionary significance. Childhood and the family are themselves historical variables and it seems that the principle of setting aside a part of early life that is given over to fantasy, detachment from more demanding aspects of 'reality' and simple enjoyment of the powers of imagination for their own sake, is something that emerges only with a distinctively modern, perhaps even romantic, notion of childhood (Postman 1985). Such a period of personal exploration and indulgence seems to be functional for personal development in a capitalist society, although its benefits were initially reserved for bourgeois children and only extended to the rest of society in the twentieth century. For much of the modern period play has produced individuals who have learned the physical principles of life in a world shaped by industry; acquired an intelligent conformism to the codified demands of authority, and possess an over-arching sense of social solidarity.

In this account play is related, in all of its dimensions, to the idea of learning as a positive good that is fundamental to social development. Through play we get individuals who are able to participate as citizens and have acquired the competencies basic to civilized life. The level of education and skill of individuals in the population is closely tied into the level of development of the social formation as a whole and playing games is an essential part of this education process. A society that fails to educate will be one that falls behind. Technology, therefore, was always a part of play. Leather footballs, the organisation of fields into pitches, playing pieces on marked boards, wooden hoops and model railways all illustrate this. Such toys are not simply about representing the world to children, they also include giving them a feel for it, introducing some of its technical principles and preparing them for some relationship to the means of production.

There is some consensus among theorists of play that it is a near-universal phenomenon which, to some extent, eludes the 'rational nexus' (Huizinga 1938: 3) that grounds most interpretation in the human sciences. People everywhere do it and its purposes and significance are always somewhat enigmatic. Johann Huizinga

---

[1] I recently watched my son befriend another child at the 'Game On' computer games exhibition, Barbican Centre, London Summer 2002, in order that they could challenge each other's mastery of 'Pokémon' characters. Incidentally, Kline *et al*'s claim (2003: 254) that Pokémon is a violent game strikes me as quite absurd.

and Roger Caillois, the main theorists of play until recent times, converge on some defining properties of play, all of which relate to computer games. They agree that play is always voluntary – we cannot be forced to play, without compromising the very nature of the activity. Similarly, both agree that play is an activity that is separate from the rest of life; it goes on in a discrete place and time that has been set aside for the purpose. Play is also always open in terms of its outcomes, whether this is because we may have more or less skill than an opponent or just a matter of luck, as in card games, the results of play are never completely known in advance. Significantly, both thinkers describe play as essentially unproductive, unlike other areas of human endeavour that involve concentration and effort. Play, according to Caillois can be open and unstructured but playing games always involves rules. In computer games these will be implemented in the game algorithm. Finally, and perhaps most significantly, both thinkers converge on the essential role of make believe in play. Play involves willed departure from the real world and into one whose parameters are determined by imagination, including collective or joint imaginings. In this respect, play is fundamentally linked by Caillois to the wearing of masks and to the assuming of roles (See Huizinga 1938: 8-15; Caillois 1958: 31-42).

Both Huizinga and Caillois also maintain that play has what they term a 'civilizing function'. This relates to the idea that play is related to core learning processes, essential to the survival and cultural reproduction of societies. Societies that do not play, or where play is engineered rather than entered into freely, will ultimately descend into barbarism and cultural decay. For Huizinga, the role of play in pitching us against one another in combat, which we can win only through courage and endurance, is essential. Play, like virtue, requires courage and a kind of inner hardness: 'To dare, to take risks, to bear uncertainty, to endure tension – these are the essence of the play spirit.' (1938: 51) Caillois offers a differentiated conception of play, separating out the more progressive dimensions of play experience. Civilizing, or beneficial play, he suggests, consists in activity that prioritises competition (*agon*) and chance (*alea*) over the more passive forms of play. In the latter class he includes role playing (*mimicry*) and the kind of reverie (*ilinx*) associated with intense play, wherein one loses all sense of self:

> In *agon*, the player relies only upon himself and his utmost efforts; in *alea*, he counts on everything except himself, submitting to the powers that elude him; in *mimicry*, he imagines that he is someone else, and he invents an imaginary universe; in *ilinx*, he gratifies the desire to temporarily destroy his bodily equilibrium, escape the tyranny of his ordinary perception, and provoke the abdication of conscience. (Caillois 1958: 44)

In primitive, or retrogressive forms of play *mimicry* and *ilinx* dominate as play is essentially unregulated (*paidia*), childish and exuberant. As society progresses and play evolves *paidia* is differentiated by more rule-governed forms of play, associated with *agon* and *alea*. Caillois calls this higher, rule-bound form of play *ludus*. In the evolution of play, *paidia* is differentiated by *ludus*. Progress can be measured in terms of the extent to which *agon* and *alea* combined have displaced or reduced the role of *mimicry* and *ilinx* in the play of a culture. He bases this on his idea that there is a natural affinity between games of competition and games of chance, on one side, and open unstructured play on the other. Historically, there is an antipathy between the two pairs:

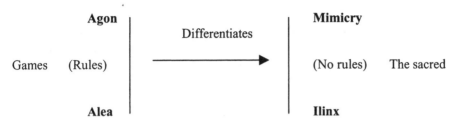

Figure 4.1: Caillois and the Evolution of Play

Although we can conceive of games that both overwhelm our senses, drawing us into the kind of reverie associated with *ilinx*, and are based on chance, the two modes of play are not overtly compatible. Moreover, Caillois says that *agon* and *ilinx* are actually incompatible. This opposition seems to be subverted by many computer games, in which players compete and yet lose themselves in an experience that many hard-core gamers call 'the zone' – an experience of timelessness that comes from absolute engagement with each passing moment of game play.[2]

In contrast, there is a natural affinity between games of competition and chance. Both involve a kind of 'pseudo-equality' that is engineered for the game world – such as agreed handicaps in golf. Both are centred on 'winning' in some sense. And both are rule-governed. This links them culturally to the rise of modern societies, in which the most important struggles are the ones with tangible outcomes, while the illusions that were once invested in sacred rites have been largely done away with. Indeed, these two dimensions of play are so closely related that most modern games involve elements of both skill and chance. Caillois discusses how, in contrast, the wearing of masks and the experience of ecstatic reverie are completely bound up with one another in societies where the sacred still holds sway and, essentially, people are subdued by false idols. Ultimately, this is because role play and religious ecstacy are passive pleasures, whereas *agon* and *alea* involve us actively. The latter drive cultures that are on the road to enlightenment, while *mimicry* and *ilinx* predominate in cultures that are sunk in themselves. I am not convinced that such retrograde cultures exist or have ever existed. However, the idea of play as a cultural form that differentiates itself in this way resonates with the emphasis placed above on the relationship between play and learning processes that mark social advance. It might be usefully incorporated into Habermas's conception of social evolution as the progressive differentiation of social

---

[2] 'Ikaruga', a game by Treasure software, for the Nintendo Gamecube, is a game that cannot be played well without encountering an experience of this kind. I am grateful to Bruce Brodie for fascinating discussions of this.

functions in a manner consistent with the human refusal to not-learn (Habermas 1979: 15; See also Kirkpatrick 2003 for further discussion of this). This perspective is useful when distinguishing the merits of different games and their relation to the evolution of a specific culture; it is perhaps less useful as a way of comparing levels of development between different societies or cultures. The point of this as an element in critical theory would be to highlight defects in the normal functioning of play as a social mechanism, relative to its failure to deliver learning outcomes that correspond to the evolutionary needs of society.

Ludology

When assessing the cultural significance of the computer game it is obviously correct that we should assess it primarily in terms of its effects on play. This view has been argued most forcefully by a Scandinavian school of thinkers known as ludologists. From this standpoint, the evaluative standards we should apply to computer games come from the players' perspective. When we assess games we should not be primarily interested in their aesthetic qualities (are they 'realistic', good simulations, beautiful experiences etc.) but their 'playability'. We should not focus on their narrative content, but what they are like to play. Ludologists have dedicated their energies to developing a set of principles and criteria that can be used to interpret, analyse and critically assess computer games from this perspective. Insisting on the independence of play as a field of enquiry with its own emerging methodological and criteriological standards, ludologists have also generated some meta-level reflection on the nature of play in modern culture. Bo Kampmann Walther's (2003) reflections on methodology fall into this category and are useful to any attempt to clarify what is specific to play with computer games.

Walther distinguishes between play and game rather differently than Caillois. In play, he writes, 'the deep fascination lies in the oscillation between play and non-play,' whereas in the playing of games we are fixated on progressing within the prior structure that is the game. Play is always defined by a tension, in which we constantly resist falling out of the fantasy context of play and back into reality. But when play is focused on a game, the tension is between success and failure in our achievement of defined objectives. Walther argues that in all play there is an 'initial transgression', whereby we move from the mundane world of existence into the play world. Once there we partake of a prevailing 'unreality' which demands our attention. This can be followed by a second transgression, which takes us into the game world proper, a further, false reality to which we commit in full knowledge of its falsity. In playing a computer game we work within a second 'as if structure' overlain on top of the first. Maintaining these willed illusions involves us in intense, serious concentration – features of play already well understood by Huizinga and Caillois. However, it also involves a certain self-understanding; players know that they are responsible for maintaining the illusion that is the game world and the sense of play that supports it. This knowledge ultimately threatens the game and play itself, giving it a kind of ontological insecurity. This is why play is often repetitive, since repetition reinforces the reality of the game world (Huizinga 1938: 10). However, this same repetitiveness results in a kind of disenchantment for the player (essentially, it is not fun) and an inability on her part to continue 'foregrounding' the game play experience. Awareness of broader reality resurfaces with the result that we 'fall out of character' and 'lose touch'. At this point the player 'fail[s] to sense a presence from the inside of presence's deterritorialisation' (Walther 2003). There is an exhaustion of the possibilities of the game and the only way to re-enter game play proper is to invent new rules for subsequent engagement; to innovate.

One of the many points of interest in this theorisation of the computer gaming situation is the almost complete absence of narrative as a factor informing the play experience. As ludology has asserted the originality of computer games and the necessity of establishing a new disciplinary context for game criticism, so ludologists have turned away from narrative and literary theory as methodologies. This is exactly what the perspective of critical technology, and that of new media as theorised by Manovich would anticipate. The experience of playing a game has much more to do with negotiating a database through a complex series of interactions with a parser, or algorithm, than it has to do with the demands of negotiating, or even constructing a narrative. At the heart of game play is a uniquely un-mediated sensation of the technical, an opening up of the body to the rhythm and pace of the machine in an experience that is neither preceded by a technical understanding of what is happening, nor mediated by any narrative construction put upon it by the game interface. Another leading ludologist, Espen Aarseth sums up this, central characteristic of computer games when he says that they make the player a target of a vicious set of contrivances, or of a 'computer generated intrigue' (Aarseth 1997: 114). All computer games are, in this sense, dynamic puzzles. Playing them requires not only a willing suspension of disbelief, but 'willing suspension of one's normal capacity for language, physical aptness, and social interaction as well' (Aarseth 1997: 117).

Building on his characterisation of the essential structure of the computer in terms of its database-algorithm architecture, discussed in the last chapter, Manovich argues that the computer game stands between two conflicting forces in contemporary culture. On one side, the computer offers us a way of experiencing meaning that is based on lists and data structures. This stands opposed to narrative, which is the dominant way of experiencing meaning in pre-digital societies. The majority of computer games seem to offer meaningful contexts of engagement ordered, ostensibly at least, after the fashion of a traditional, linear narrative. That is to say that the games introduce stories and invite us to participate in them. This participation may be expected to uncover further information relevant to the story (back-story) and it will invariably carry the story forward towards some kind of resolution. In a game, players interact with a database of images and messages by affecting state changes in a parser – an instruction set containing conditional (if-then) statements, targeted on user input. In this way, each player negotiates an individual course through some of the items in the database and, in so doing, generates a narrative kind of experience. Although the narrative aspect is clearly important to games – they can be seen as interactive stories – it is important for Manovich that, '…database and narrative do not have the same status in computer culture… a database can support narrative, but there is nothing in the logic of the medium itself that would foster its generation' (Manovich 2001: 228). Moreover, the two aspects of the medium are inherently antagonistic:

> As a cultural form, the database represents the world as a list of items, and it refuses to order this list. In contrast, a narrative creates a cause-and-effect trajectory of seemingly unordered items (events). Therefore, database and narrative are natural enemies. Competing for the same territory of human culture, each claims an exclusive right to make meaning out of the world. (Manovich 2001: 225)

This interpretation of games highlights the point made in the previous chapter, namely, that there is an innate inconsistency between attempts to simulate 'natural' contexts of human action regulated by social convention and the very different principles that govern machine behaviour. It also makes games appear as something of a transitional form, in which users experience new possibilities for meaning-creation associated with the database, packaged up as the navigation of virtual space, or the interactive construction of a personalised fictional narrative.

The computer game is not alone in this balancing of the traditional and the new. Most new media, Manovich writes, involve us in a kind of oscillation between gathering information and acting on it:

> …as the user keeps checking whether the information is coming, she actually addresses the machine itself. The machine reveals itself; it reminds the user of its existence – not only because the user is forced to wait but also because she is forced to witness how the message is being constructed over time. A page fills in part by part, top to bottom; text comes before images; images arrive in low resolution and are gradually refined. Finally, everything comes together in a smooth sleek image – the image that will be destroyed with the next click. (Manovich 2001: 206)

This movement between two action orientations, or temperaments – the one passive and accepting, the other active and engaged – is definitive of all work with a PC interface, but its purest exemplar is the computer game. Players of computer games must oscillate between acting on the game world and periods when they are assimilating information and working out what they have to do next to effect relevant state changes in the machine. They cannot, therefore, suspend disbelief and immerse themselves in the game completely for protracted periods of time without being interrupted by the fact that their pleasure presupposes, or is produced by, a machine. Here it is not the machine as database that is prioritised, but its algorithmic character:

> The similarity between the actions expected of the player and computer algorithms is too uncanny to be dismissed. While computer games do not follow a database logic, they appear to be ruled by another logic – that of the algorithm. They demand that a player execute an algorithm in order to win… As the player proceeds through the game, she gradually discovers the rules that operate in the universe constructed by this game. She learns its hidden logic – in short, its algorithm. (Manovich 2001: 222)

On this account, the game player is engaged in an unconscious process of internalising the workings of a computer program and, if she is playing successfully, having her own actions dictated by them. This does not restore us to the notion of a single linear course through each game database, rather, it defers the element of player navigation to specific points in the interactive sequence, possibly against the background of a persistent context of play, possibly involving those theorised by Walther as moments of disengagement from the game, complete detachment and the search for innovation. At the heart of these theorisations of computer game play is the idea of oscillation as the physical playing out of computer imposed routines, or algorithms. As Turkle writes, 'The video games reflect the computer within – in their animated graphics, in the rhythm they impose, in the kind of strategic thinking that they require' (Turkle 1984: 62). While Manovich acknowledges that the oscillation he describes '...is not an artefact of computer technology but a structural feature of modern society' (2001: 209), his interpretation of the relevant ideological context is, as noted in the previous chapter, largely uncritical. To understand the appeal of the computer game and its relationship to the PC interface we need to grasp the mass psychology of play in the post-cold war era.

The Cynicism of the Computer Gamer

Computer games commonly hold out the possibility of excitement, adventure and fulfilment through action in an environment where even the most fantastic narrative contexts are brought to life. However, advocates of computer games as legitimate sources of meaning in contemporary cultural life rarely pretend that this narrative context, or dramatic setting is ever as rich, or as diverse in terms of its interactive possibilities, as other symbolically mediated contexts of action. Sherry Turkle, who, as seen in the previous chapter, repeatedly overstates the autonomy of the interface as a cultural artefact from its machinic underpinnings, acknowledges that:

> Current video games are still recognisably rule-based, although they are... sophisticated, with more random elements and branching points. (1996: 67)

The point is perhaps most clearly illustrated by those games that are punctuated by short clips of non-interactive video-style film, describing a series of events that link one stage in a game to another. As Steven Poole writes, these are useful devices if they help to maintain the illusion and keep the player involved, but 'The unique pleasure of a videogame..., the one that no other medium can offer, is always going to be what happens between the episodes of the story' (Poole 2000: 123).

The narrative possibilities of the computer game are limited by the branching algorithms that underpin the alternatives available to players at any given time. It does not follow from this that computer game play is necessarily devoid of subjective meaning-content. As Turkle writes, 'there is nothing mindless about mastering a video game' (1984: 61), in fact, she argues, computer games, '...put... people into a highly focused, and highly charged state of mind' (1984: 79). But this state of mind is different to the willed suspension of disbelief associated with theatre-going. It is interactive, but in a very specific, even historically unique sense:

> ...in order for you to play successfully, the general principles, like the patterns, have to be more than memorised. It's more than thinking – in a way it's beyond thinking. The hand learns what to do and does it automatically... (Turkle 1984: 62)

Having initially been seduced by the game's interface, the successful player, must 'see through it' in order to defeat the machine and progress through the levels. However, the appeal of the game's interface is, in the manner of all seductions, based on a kind of deceit. In the case of computer games this deceit concerns the true character of the narrative context that the user is being asked to enter. There is no shortage of comments in interface design literature to support the idea that designers see themselves as involved in an activity with social consequences as profound as any statecraft, and as employed in the routine deceit of people who *want* to be deceived. Brenda Laurel, for instance, argues that the secret to good interface design is to control what users will do with the machine through clever use of implicit constraints rather than explicit injunctions on certain actions (1993: 105). In a similar vein, Turkle observes that when playing with their computers people, '...suspend disbelief and become absorbed in what is happening on the screen' (Turkle 1996: 103). To play a game is to be seduced by the illusion that what is happening at the interface is a self-sufficient context of action; that it is worth engaging with the machine at the level of the narrative context the game seems to offer us.[3]

As Walther's discussion highlights, however, the illusory game world is not stable, it resides in a tension between the player's willed transgression in play and their life in the mundane world. Indeed, the most intense experiences of play with games presuppose moments of detachment and even complete disengagement on the part of their players. What is curious about computer game play seems to be this oscillation between the two modes, or action orientations – the one suspended, deceived, the other disengaged and yet persistent in working through the physical actions associated with play. Those who continue to 'play' beyond the point just described, which includes most of us and all 'successful' players, do so even though the pleasurable, entertainment value of the game has evaporated. We play in spite of, and in full cognisance of, the absence of any sense of play.[4] This affords us a sense of mastery, but at the same time dispels the illusion that made us want it in the first place. We end up mastering something that no longer matters to us. A machine-imposed choreography takes over from thought in determining our movements so

---

[3] That players want to be seduced is fairly clear from Poole's comment that, '...if prescripted story scenes can enhance this feeling of involvement, then they serve a useful purpose... but we don't want to have to make crucial narrative decisions...' (Poole 2000: 123).

[4] Poole argues that computer games occupy the unique place they do in Japanese culture partly because there is a tradition there of holding the form of an activity in esteem for its own sake, regardless of content (2000: 166).

that we effectively surrender our bodies to the machine.[5] The computer games player is forced into awareness that his activity is merely a codified response to machine implemented algorithms. Rather than use this awareness, however, the cynical player accepts his status as mere connector in an electronically determined circuit. He sees the truth but surrenders to the hold of the interface regardless.

The cynical consciousness is one that reaches an understanding or insight into the nature of phenomenon but does not act on that insight if action involves a challenge to power. This aligns the consciousness of the computer game player with the cynicism diagnosed in Cold War Europe by Peter Sloterdijk, at the very time the first games were spreading across the continent. Describing the mood of 'sullen withdrawal' that prevailed at this time, Sloterdijk writes:

Cynicism is enlightened false consciousness. It is that modernised, unhappy consciousness on which Enlightenment has laboured both successfully and in vain. It has learned its lessons in enlightenment but it has not, and probably was not able to, put them into practice. Well-off and miserable at the same time, this consciousness no longer feels affected by any critique of ideology; its falseness is already reflexively buffered. (Sloterdijk 1987: 5)

The games player is both naïve and enlightened. He learns the truth that the games interface is simply a deception, irrelevant to successful play, and makes this knowledge the basis for successful play. He feels the rhythms of the machine and the underlying algorithms of the game program as they play out through his body – the game plays him – and reaches the awareness that these operations are devoid of meaning. In this way, games play leaves us poised on the edge of enlightenment about the underlying character of the game's reality and yet too enlightened to do anything about it, as we can see that this would require work and engagement with the technical while we are here to 'play'. Like Sloterdijk's cynics, we are in possession of an effective 'ideology-critique' but not motivated to act on the underlying reality, preferring instead to keep 'playing the game'. As Poole writes, '...the player is a happy slave...' (Poole 2000: 123).

Manovich also understands the appeal of the game interface in terms of a kind of public cynicism. Describing contemporary ideology, he writes:

The ideology does not demand that the subject blindly believe it, as it did in the early twentieth century; rather, it puts the subject in the master position of someone who knows very well that she is being fooled, and generously lets herself be fooled. (Manovich 2001: 209)

However, he does not see that such an attitude corresponds, not to a new empowerment of the masses, but to practical paralysis. The central oversight in Manovich's account of games is his neglect of the constraining role of the

---

[5] The most extreme illustration of this is provided by the 'cyberobics' games, discussed by Critser (2003: 168), in which players gyrate, mesmerised, in front of their screens in the attempt to lose weight.

interface. While he grasps the cynical disposition rather well, he is wrong to say that it is control that attracts the player. It is the illusion of control and the temptations of ownership. He is wrong to say that,

> ...the user is put in a much stronger position of mastery than ever before when she is 'deconstructing' commercials, newspaper reports of scandals, and other traditional noninteractive media. The user invests in the illusion precisely because she is given control over it. (Manovich 2001: 209)

The element of seduction highlights the fact that what is being withheld from users is as important as what is being given them by the games interface. Viewed in terms of the sociological model of play elaborated above, computer games take us to the brink of introducing cognitive capacities that might enable us to participate more effectively in networked society. They make us feel the underlying, algorithmic character of the computer. But they are usually designed to inhibit us from actually acquiring these competencies. This design is even manifest in the controls that players use to act upon the machine. Whereas PC users may gain access to hidden levels of their machines using the keyboard and screen, the gamer may be limited to using a 'joy-stick'.[6] The computer game prepares its players for a life operating graphical user interfaces, but not for a future in electronic engineering or programming. We are inoculated against learning about the material basis of life in networked society and, as the comments above on the 'hard knocks' of traditional play indicate, this is a peculiar deficiency, specific to the play of our time. Computer games playing fosters cynical enlightenment in place of education.

The notion that game playing is a form of cynicism enables us to situate the computer game as a cultural force, against the background of the cold war. According to Sloterdijk, hardness and conflict served to define reality itself for modern subjects; until the 1980s we ordered the ontological magnitude of things by analysing their proximity to the painful and the violent. Consequently, he argues that,

> War is the backbone of the conventional reality principle. With all its burdening consequences for the construction of social institutions, it represents the innermost, most bitter core of experience of life in class societies... (Sloterdijk 1987: 323)

In seeking to confirm one representation of the world as more 'real' than another, our strategy was always to ascertain whether the world it depicts is true to our most profound experiences. For modern subjects, these were the experiences of war, violence and death.[7] The cynicism implicit in this observation was at work on both sides of the cold war stand-off:

---

[6] I am grateful to J. W. G. Wilson for discussion of this point.

[7] This is still the preferred strategy of the makers of *The Matrix* (1999). When Neo is detached from the matrix the main reason he and we accept that he is then experiencing the 'real' world for the first time is that it is such a horrible, slimy, austere and unpleasant place.

...the conflict confronts a socialism that practices more exploitation than capitalism (in order to hinder the latter) with a capitalism that is more socialist than socialism (in order to hinder the latter)....Relaxation of tension can only happen as an uncramping from within, that is, as *insight* into the fact that the only thing we have to lose is the unbearable, armed illusion of a difference between systems. (Sloterdijk 1987: 247-8)

On each side, those who worked for the system did not believe any more in its ideology. Functionaries of the Soviet state did not believe that it was socialist and advocates of capitalism were similarly insincere in their advocacy of that system. Yet both sets of players continued, despite their enlightenment about their own system, in their efforts to build war machines capable of destroying the other several times over.

Sloterdijk's characterisation of the historical context within which computer games first became important discloses the full historical significance of the computer game as the source of a different, softer reality principle. In Sloterdijk's analysis, only a new reality principle could unlock the cold war. The computer game precipitated, perhaps even caused just such a softening. This was not achieved through rational insight, as Sloterdijk anticipated (1987: 129) but rather through deterritorialisation of militaristic, disciplined and paranoid attitudes and behaviour into a new realm of play where, as we have seen, enlightenment was suspended without being negated.[8] The objective social function of the computer game as a form of play has been to cause the kind of relaxation of tension that Sloterdijk called for: 'If we do not learn... to create soft facts by means of a new principle of reality and rationality, it could be that in the near future the hard facts will see to our downfall' (Sloterdijk 1987: 325).

As we have seen, game play is associated with the creation of an imaginary world that runs parallel to the real. Computer games provide objectifications of the imaginary world of play, enabling us to share the play world as a public representation. The emergence of a culture of play around the computer and of a widespread willingness on the part of adults to participate in constructing such environments together must be understood in the context of this need for 'soft facts', and not as the inevitable outcome of technology, or of developments in media.[9] The clamouring for 'virtual' environments reflects a social need with specific historical origins. In the games interface, phenomenal aspects of the virtual world are tailored to match perfectly the needs of the human eye and our other sensory apparatus. For millennia, our sensory apparatus evolved to adapt us to reality, now we bring salient features of it into line with the requirements of our

---

[8] The shift being described here is not without historical precedent. Huizinga notes that in traditional play seriousness and play are fluid in relation to each other. What Sloterdijk calls our 'inner hardness' is captured well in Huizinga's characterisation of the attitude that accompanies all play: 'To dare, to take risks, to bear uncertainty, to endure tension – these are the essence of the play spirit' (1950: 51).

[9] Tim Jordan's discussion of the ilinx-like reverie at the heart of the 1990s dance culture is also relevant here (Jordan 2002: 92-3).

senses.[10] This is the creation of soft facts, generated for a cynical consciousness that knows they are illusions but also knows that the price of acting on that knowledge is too high.

Play and Ideology

The computer game has acted as a kind of cultural battering ram for the idea of the computer as a small, personal machine that could be pleasurable to use. It has normalised the idea of the computer as a technological medium, making the principles of real time interaction, using simple controls, and relating to on-screen imagery in an appropriately engaged kind of way into a well-recognised behavioural syntax. Quoting Brian Winston, Kline *et al* point out that '...video games are a spin-off of the computer that in a way 'happened in advance of the parent device', since in their early days the diffusion of consoles outstripped that of personal computers, which are usually considered the centrepiece of the information revolution' (2003: 68). Machines like the Spectrum ZX and the Commodore, manufactured in the late 1970s and early 1980s, were widely perceived as gaming machines, although they were strictly speaking personal computers, and they rapidly out-sold their more work-related rivals (Edge 2003).

The first computer game, 'Space War' was invented by hackers at MIT in 1962. The game became the first arcade game in 1971, with the name 'Computer Space'. The industry grew rapidly for the next decade and by the late 1970s, games had penetrated the cultural mainstream with 'Space Invaders' in 1978, and arcade classics like 'Centipede', 'Joust' and others. The computer game is now comparable to film in its economic, as well as its cultural importance. The medium includes arcade games, games for PCs and games that are played on home consoles. The giant games corporations (Nintendo, Microsoft and Sony) compete for share of a market worth $30 billion in 1999 (Kline *et al* 2003: 12) – the comparable figure for the movie industry in the same year was $47.9 billion. While the market for games has been teenage males for most of the industry's existence, there is evidence that this demographic is changing, with female gamers becoming increasingly numerous. According to some sources more than 60% of games are purchased by people over 18, with people older than 30 accounting for a third of the market in the US (Poole 2000). Kline *et al* argue that the computer game is the ideal commodity for informational capitalism – a kind of metonym for the system as a whole (Cf Gere 2003: 178). There are a number of senses in which this claim makes sense.

As seen in chapter two, informationalism requires increasingly flexible production. Short, targeted runs based on optimal sourcing and targeted at market segments identified in advance have enabled capitalist players to exploit information processing techniques associated with networked computing. Whereas

---

[10] In this sense, the computer game is the game of all games: 'Into an imperfect world and into the confusion of life it [play] brings a temporary, limited perfection' (Huizinga 1938: 10).

capitalism in most of the Twentieth Century managed demand by creating desire for products well in advance, especially through the use of mass media advertising campaigns, informationalism tends to identify markets by researching what people want today and then bringing it to them tomorrow. According to Kline *et al*, computer game marketing has been at the leading edge of this kind of marketing from its inception:

> Video game marketers and cultural intermediaries strive to infiltrate every cultural space where young consumers might hang out, from multiplex cinemas showing 'Tomb Raider' movies to Sega theme parks to Nintendo-sponsored snowboarding terrain parks… (2003: 73)

The need to respond immediately to the demands of a rapidly changing youth market means that the games industry is highly unstable. A few wrong decisions in a short period of time can bring large organisations to their knees. In 1981 Atari found themselves ploughing thousands of game cartridges into the desert (Kent 2001), while a few years later Nintendo and Sega segmented their markets on the basis of an age differential of less than two years, with Nintendo the system of choice for younger players.

Informationalism is a globalising economic system that relies upon the spread of networked computer technology. The broader the reach of the network the greater leverage information gives in the pursuit of competitiveness. The computer game has spear-headed the global reach of digital technology. As Nicholas Garnham points out: 'videogame industries like Nintendo and Sega were in fact the first companies which could be said to have created a successful and global multimedia product market' (Quoted in Kline *et al* 2003: 75). This gives games an especially important role in driving the development of the new, informational economy throughout the 1980s and 90s. Games have, in a sense, made computer technology recognisable in its friendly and colourful form all over the planet. Informationalism presupposes a population that knows how to operate networked PCs. In the era of the hegemonic interface this involves familiarity with computer-generated environments that are welcoming and, of course, controlling.

The role of the computer game in the development of the hegemonic interface discussed in the previous chapter has been threefold. First, many of the aesthetic principles that have been implemented in user friendly interfaces originated in graphical innovations associated with games. As Manovich points out (2001: 244), the computer game is almost certainly the most advanced form of meaning production and circulation using digital technology. As the pioneer and emissary of digital culture, the central motif of the computer game is the navigation of virtual space. The ideas of construing interfaces on the model of theatre and of creating 2 and 3-D environments that involve users in step by step 'walkthroughs' to achieve predetermined objectives, originate with and are most thoroughly explored in computer games. Games also foster demand for 'more and better' of these graphical interface phenomena. It has been widely observed that recent developments in PC technology, including memory expansion slots, higher resolution displays and enhanced sound facilities, are generally of limited benefit to the casual PC user. It is as a gaming machine that the PC really benefits from such enhancements and they are generally marketed first to PC users who play games on their machines. Finally, games have served to normalise the idea of the computer as a source of friendly, exciting and 'fun' illusions. Ideas like 'virtuality' and 'interactivity' have been promoted in connection with a certain, essentially unchallenging class of experiences associated with PC use. In this sense, computer games train people for life in a society dominated by computer technology.

> Video and computer games embody the new forces of production, consumption and communication with which capital is once again attempting to force itself beyond its own limits to commodify life with a new scope and identity; they play a crucial role in a digital transformation of the texture and processes of everyday life; they typify the strategies and imperatives of the new regime of accumulation marked by increased reliance on simulations both as work tools and as consumer commodities. Indeed, as many information age pundits have suggested, video-game play can be seen as a sort of low-level domestic socialisation for high-tech work practices. (Kline *et al* 2003: 76)

This critique highlights the ways in which the computer game has been and continues to be functional for informational capitalism – a system which, despite all the hype about 'knowledge working' and the need for 'lifelong learning' has an at best contradictory relationship to learning as an indicator of social progress. As such, it complements the critique developed here of the 'friendly interface' that limits us to taking ownership of virtual environments, while prohibiting us from acquiring the technical skills necessary really to control them. We can mix our labour with the virtual objects but we cannot determine the rules of their behaviour, what they mean, or what the consequences of all this information processing will be. Play with games trains us for this by inculcating cynical resignation as the habitual form of work with graphical interfaces.

This aligns the computer game with a specific temperament that is determinate for the computer culture and which plays a role in the technical politics in which we contest the PC and its interface. The cynicism of the computer gamer is that attitude of resignation to the failure of the interface and the gaze that sees right through it but carries on playing regardless. The attitude of the worker who drags and drops for twenty minutes when she knows a command line would do it all in a flash, but does not know what the command is, or how to access the relevant interface, and does not care. This is not the same thing as a critique of game content. Here it is important that game narratives are, at best, relatively unimportant to the game player's experience of games and game play. For although the player sees through the story that made her want to play the game in the first place, the rediscovery of the spirit of play in the context of rapid fire puzzle solving in which she pits herself against the machine over and over again, is not a bad thing or one that might be expected to have retrograde consequences in itself.

Kline *et al* argue that games have reinforced negative ideological tendencies associated with capitalist patriarchy, nurturing and encouraging a kind of masculinity that invests value in violence and in the capacity for violence. But this is a superficial reading on two counts. First, the fact that many games have violence as a part of their narrative theme – the thing that makes players want to play in the first place – is a function of the broader culture and not the game medium. As Manovich points out, '...the end of the cold war played an important role in the extension of the military mode of perception into general culture.' (Manovich 2001: 277). Similarly, Slavoj Zizek notices the same torsion in our experience when he comments that the appeal of war games is not that they offer an escapist fantasy that shields us from real killing, but rather that their simulated horrors enable us to experience killing rather than 'the real of the depersonalised war turned into an anonymous technological apparatus.' (2000: 34). In other words, the fact that we want to experience conflict is a testimony to our human instinct to prefer reality over an informationalised world in which 'real' actions are increasingly mediated by soft facts (icons we click that make people in other countries redundant, or sell weapons to dictators). Interestingly, Zizek links this directly to the cynicism of contemporary politicians.

Secondly, the context into which the computer game exploded, as described by Sloterdijk, is a redefinition of conventions around public 'fun':

> For a long time now carnival has meant not 'inverted world' but flight into a safe world, or anaesthesia from a permanently inverted world full of daily absurdities. We know that, at least since Hitler, Bohemianism is dead, and in its offshoots in the subcultures cheeky moods are to be found less than cheerless attitudes of withdrawal (Sloterdijk 1987: 118).

It is in this context that we should assess the claims and counter-claims about computer game violence. The computer game interface is about warding off the cynical moment, the point at which the player becomes detached and reduced to repeating the same movements in an effort to get past the current obstacle, even though she no longer cares what the obstacle is or why her character is trying to get past it. The most effective strategy with which to ward off the cynical attitude is to pack the interface with content that is shocking, disrespectful and subversive of established codes of conduct. As we will see in the next chapter, the opposite to cynicism is not naïve optimism but the politics of the well-timed, cheeky gesture. The game interface has to mediate between the temperament of resigned, contemptuous passivity and that of adolescent mis-behaviour if it is to sustain the tension that supports the game world.

Viewed in this way, it is clear that just as computer games are primarily about play and not narrative meaning, so the violence in computer games is less about real violence than it is about cynicism as a computational temperament. In traditional play, fighting within the rules of good conduct was the definition of virtue. Committing, or chancing one's self within the rules of combat against a respected opponent is a cultural universal, in which 'the innate human need of rhythm, harmony, change, alternation, combat and climax etc. [can] unfold in full richness' (1938: 75). Huizinga suggests that this is linked to the carnivalesque, the orgiastic frenzies of the popular masses throughout the medieval period. In the modern era, though, the spirit of play has tended to get smothered under, 'a rank layer of ideas, systems of thought and knowledge, doctrines, rules and regulations, moralities and conventions which have all lost touch with play' (1938: 75). The excessive violence of the computer game world reflects the violence with which the genuinely popular and playful in culture have been suppressed. It is not in itself violent, so much as deliberately celebratory of the controversial and provocative. This interpretation resonates with the, albeit limited, ethnographic literature on game play, which shows gamers to be wry, humorous and cheeky in relation to each other and their games, rather than in the grip of any malign or paranoid sentiments (Wright *et al* 2002). At the same time, violence in games reflects the powerlessness of the gamer to bring about any real change, to actually resurrect the spirit of carnival, or of popular culture in the age of mass media.

Conclusion

In traditional play the technological component was incidental. This is no longer the case. Computer games playing is something that people enter into with a completely different sense of the underlying physical and technical reality than was ever the case in the era of playing 'boards' or pogo sticks. The physical reality of toys certainly had cultural meaning, but this symbolic aspect would recede once play proper had commenced. With computer games this dynamic is reversed. Just as with traditional toys, the appropriate 'playful' orientation to a technical device such as a play station or gamecube is something that has to be learned. Only people who have encountered interfaces before and who recognise the need to commit, imaginatively to the world represented there will be able to participate. We have to learn to see past the technology to suspend our reservations about it and enter the game. With computer games, however, the hold of the game world is inherently unstable and as shallow in its hold on the player's imagination as it is elaborate in its narrative, or world-simulating complexity. Reference to game objectives as portrayed in the interface narrative becomes shorthand for the mastery of generic, technical controls. In particular, what the player does is self-consciously interact with a technical system, without allowing the knowledge that it is a technical system to affect their interaction with it. On one hand, this represents a migration of technology and the technical to the centre of the subjective experience of play.[11] But on the other, gaming leaves us suspended on the brink of real knowledge, taking ownership of but never actually controlling the 'virtual' gaming environment.

While they deny us access to the kind of reflexive understanding of technology that this book argues is essential in the information age, games can be used as pedagogic aids. By linking information to enjoyment, computer game play offers

---

[11] As Poole writes, '...you can play chess with bits of mud, or foorball with scrunched up newspaper and a few sweaters, you cannot play a modern videogame without a machine' (2000: 173).

much potential to educators and this has been explored by a number of pioneering researchers. For all this, however, the contemporary computer game is an illusion that induces cynicism about the technology itself. Games train us for life in a society which now possesses a 'soft factual' basis. We affect real changes by 'clicking' on 'teleactive' icons (Manovich 2001: 170) and, as Sean Cubitt writes, 'What changes is the experiential quality of work' (Cubitt 2000: 90). The idea that this change should lead us to revise our basic ontology is problematic, as we saw in the last chapter. Reality is still hard and it is probably still physical. It is true that through the 'teleactive power of the image' we can affect real change merely by acting upon symbolic representations, but this was always true. Typists, bureaucrats and all previous information workers have done the same thing. What changes in informationalism is the aesthetics – the feel of the world – and the speed with which symbolic re-orderings can be translated into actions with real consequences. We do not lose the distinction between reality and sign, but the propensity for acting upon the world through the medium of signs is enhanced in its aesthetic significance and its material importance.

In this and in other ways too, computer games are contradictory. The temperament associated with game play is not progressive in any traditional sense of that term – games do not produce a communicative action orientation and they essentially pin us down to physically determined patterns of behaviour based on trivial algorithms. At the same time, this attitude produces a kind of relaxation of tension in the public sphere – the very opposite effect to that which is claimed by critics of 'violent' content – of the kind that Sloterdijk anticipated might be produced through an effort of collective rationality. Instead, this relaxation seems to have been brought about through a revival of the spirit of play. Viewed in this way, the left-wing critique of game violence – 'militarised masculinity' (Kline *et al* 2003) – misses the point, since the reality of gaming has little to do with actual violence, something a five minute encounter with any hard core gamer would confirm. Indeed, it seems more likely that games have helped save the world from unthinkable violence by making that violence 'real'. Certainly this is more plausible than the claim that they have made the world more violent by encouraging us to experience it (violence) in 'unreal' form.

This chapter has situated the computer game in relation to the sociology and politics of the PC interface, which is one aspect of the struggle for hegemony over technology design in the digital era. Viewed in this way, the computer game is a cultural form that is functional for informational capitalism. It fosters the development of increasingly seductive and opaque interfaces on technology, has led the way in the development of global digital cultural production and provides training for life in a society that is increasingly mediated by intelligent, 'friendly' technology. In this chapter I have stressed that play with computer games includes at its core a distinctive temperament or attitude of mind. This corresponds to a culturally dominant disposition, which is that of knowing resignation, or cynicism. It is this cynicism that explains the seeming violence of computer games and which is key to understanding the modern experience of play and the demand for play with computers. Although this seems like a negative interpretation of the game play phenomenon, I have also emphasised that left wing cultural critics have been too quick to dismiss the game, and gamers, on the basis of superficial affinities with negative elements in 'mass culture'. In fact, the game is a contradictory cultural form. Games can be interpreted as stupefying, pacifying and diverting – as an ideological commodity. Intense game play, however, takes us into a physical experiencing of the routines of the machine that dominates modern life. Play with computer games introduces us to the aesthetics of existence in networked society. Through this kind of play we learn the rules of participation in interface culture and computer-mediated communication. There is a sense, then, in which the computer gamer can be described as the true owner of 'virtual' space. He has made it his own. However, ownership and control have been separated out in the digital era, by the intervention of the interface level. If the gamer owns the interface like no other user, it is the hacker who controls what they experience when they are there.

Chapter 5

Hacking as 'Thwarted Vocation'

Introduction

Computer hacking has been interpreted as a form of deviant psychology, as the product of social labelling processes and as a uniquely odious kind of criminal behaviour. It has also been read in terms of its affinities with radical strains in contemporary political culture. In this chapter, I argue that, while each of these interpretations contributes unique insights to the problem, hacking needs to be understood against the background of the social problematics of technology construction. An adequate sociology of computer hacking needs to start from the observation that the design politics of personal computing has not reached the stage of definitive closure; the form and function of the PC and of computer networks remain contested. This ongoing politics of design encompasses social structures as well as the physical constitution of the technology. All technologies go through such a period of flux in their designs, when different social forces compete to impose their interpretations of how the potential in the technology may best be used. Hegemony within the field of technology design enables some groups to establish their requirements more forcefully and successfully than others. Thereafter, finished artefacts possess that kind of unique obviousness that inheres in the technical objects we have to use in the labour process. Their operations will be nested within social and institutional practices, including the designation of some people as 'operatives', agreement on safety restrictions, and the institutionalisation of relevant kinds of expertise.

Computer hacking is a social problem because networked PCs have become fundamental economic tools in the absence of such closure in their design. In Andrew Feenberg's terms, PCs are still in flux:

> Design is only controversial when it is in flux. Resolved conflicts over technology are quickly forgotten. Their outcomes, a welter of taken-for-granted technical and legal standards, are embodied in a stable code, and form the background against which economic actors manipulate the unstable portions of the environment in the pursuit of efficiency. (Feenberg 1999: 96-7)

This continuing openness of the networked PC to conflicting interpretations and the absence of a 'stable code' that pre-structures everyone's attitude to the machine provides the indispensable sociological context for interpreting hacking and reactions to it. Codification of technology involves the imprint of a mesh of social determinants upon technical artefacts. Socially powerful groups exercise greater sway over this process than those who are marginal. Their power is wielded through the politics of design and in the creation of social structures that stabilise the final employment of the technology. Interfaces that deny people access to deeper levels of the machine and systematically preclude experimentation with it bridge the gap between these two aspects, being both technical products and social interventions.

At the same time, however, Feenberg suggests that the phase of socially determinate construction of a technology out of its raw, relatively pre-social elements also involves an integrative dimension. Technical artefacts must be things that people can use and they must fit into a prior world of experience in ways that make sense to people. We might, for example, anticipate widespread resistance to the demand that people should enter a Borg cube tomorrow and wire themselves up for a future of total agreement with the world government. 'Technique,' Feenberg writes, 'must be integrated with the natural, technical and social environments that support its functioning' (1999: 205). With any complex technical system there will be those who feel some kind of affinity with it, for whatever reason. As seen in chapter two, these people may invest values in the technology, or, quite naturally, just find themselves inexplicably drawn to it. In the process that Feenberg theorises as 'secondary instrumentalisation', such individuals are said to have a 'vocation' and social structures will evolve to harness this affinity to the social good – through the creation of professional associations and the assignment of such institutions to various kinds of regulatory role. In what follows, I will argue that such an affinity exists between hackers and computers and that the absence of social structures that reflect and accommodate this are a significant part of the explanation for hacking. Interfaces that inhibit the natural technical relation between human and machine are to be read in this light.

The absence of these structures itself traces to the fact that the systems sphere of contemporary society has over-reached itself in trying to appropriate networked PC technology in the absence of agreement on important issues. This has led to the criminalization of 'hackers' on one side and to the development of an economically significant computer security industry on the other. Both are symptomatic of the absence of consensus and closure concerning the technology and the social relationships it supports. Hacking is interpreted here as an historical temperament that has arisen in connection with the PC but is not unique to it. It has a natural origin in the relationship of human to machine and a social explanation in the attempts to stymie and corrupt this relationship. Hacking is a thwarted vocation. Its political significance does not reside in any natural affinity with so-called 'real world' politics of direct action, but in its very banality as a daily challenge to the prevailing technological hegemony.[1]

---

[1] This should not be taken as an expression of 'support' for hacking (whatever that would mean), precisely because hacking is not often politically motivated.

Secondary Instrumentalisation and the Interface

Chapter two indicated that the perspective of the original PC hackers might serve
to orientate critical theory when coming to grips with the politics of technology
and especially interface design. Chapter three suggested that critical and realist
aesthetics, consistent with this perspective, provided the basis for a critique of the
homogenising tendencies of contemporary interface design. The sumptuous, easy
to use interface deploys metaphors and images to try and create an 'environment'
within which users can orientate themselves and work out what to do next on the
basis of conventional associations that they perceive between the metaphors and
images. This aspiration sometimes succeeds; certainly it attracts people to use
computers who would otherwise be deterred by their technical complexity. At the
same time, extended use of a PC that runs Windows or provides a simulated 'desktop' environment inevitably leads people to a point at which they become
disillusioned because the standard metaphorical connections do not work. I have
found very few people who persist in thinking of their Windows screen as
providing them with a 'desktop', for instance. At various points in our experience
with even the most advanced of such interfaces we dispense with the metaphors
and easy associations and form behavioural links of our own, patterns of use that
work for us. This move is based on speculation about what the machine might do if we
try x, where x is an action on the system that is not prompted by any meaning-
contentful item on the interface. This is the beginning of hacking behaviour.

In Feenberg's terms, the early hackers were involved in the transition from
'primary' to 'secondary instrumentalisation'. The first PCs were, literally, an
assortment of technological elements, including a processor, some physical
memory and rudimentary input-output devices. They had to be 'concatenated' into
the PC form. The idea came from hobbyists and was sold to other hobbyists
through mail order. This led to an exploration of the affordances of the machine.
Steven Levy describes, for instance, the first time a hacker hobbyist discovered
that the machine could be programmed to play tunes – not something that was
designed into it beforehand (Levy 1984: 206). Through this kind of
experimentation and discovery, the assemblage of features that we now think of as
the PC was brought into being. The affordances – what the machine might be able
to do – were present in the primary instrumentalisation phase. Integrated circuits
made processors possible in the size that was necessary for personal computing,
for example. This phase generated objects that had potential for human use out of
natural raw materials – in the case of processors, silicon. The raw materials were
thereby forced into the technical relation and exposed to the technical attitude. As
seen in chapter one, people assume the minimal technological attitude by asking
what the thing can do for them, on the basis of the assumption that if they look at it
closely enough and raise appropriate hypotheses they will be able to identify
causal patterns in the behaviour of the object. Once identified, these patterns hold
the key to successful manipulation of the object towards the achievement of some
goal. The latter might be discovered by accident – the computer's beeping was an
incidental feature of the booting up process, which a hacker experimented with.

This initial wresting of objects from their natural state and their subjection to scrutiny by people looking to procure some strategic advantage from them in terms of their capacity to manipulate the world leads into secondary instrumentalisation. Secondary instrumentalisation involves the reinsertion of the object into the social and natural environment from which it was abstracted in the primary phase. This is a contradictory process because it involves harmonisation – the object must be made agreeable again, at peace with its surroundings, so to speak – but also, under capitalism at least, exploitation. In the secondary phase, the potential immanent to the PC[2] is liberated but also systematically biased, or limited in such a way as to subordinate it to the needs of money and power. This involves closing the technology off from further experimental scrutiny while it takes up its place in the systems sphere. Secondary instrumentalisation is always fraught, on Feenberg's account, because the technical relation has an immanent tendency towards integration and harmony – it involves people working with things, which, as I have argued in chapter one, is about as natural as you can get – and yet, under capitalism, this tendency always runs up against the demands of systems players that the technical be merely productive and efficient.

Feenberg argues that the aestheticised interface reflects some of these more benign aspects of technical development. He writes of '…unfriendly interfaces that emerge straight from an engineering environment alien to ordinary users…' having 'disastrous' results (1999: 124). In his discussion of the work of Winograd and Flores (1986), Feenberg suggests that the development of Artificial Intelligence as a factor in interface design may result in computers that are more readily integrated into the lifeworld experience of their human users. This is dubious, however, and there are reasons for being more circumspect[3] about the likely benefits of communicative and aesthetically pleasing interface designs that 'protect' the human being from technical complexity.

In his essay, 'Configuring the User', Steve Woolgar (Law 1991) describes the process whereby computer design began to move away from presenting their customers with 'open boxes' for experimentation and towards a more standardised presentation of the technology in different terms. He subjects the product development process in an anonymous computer firm to a critical interpretation that brings to light unacknowledged power relations. His account is based upon eighteen months as a participant-observer with the firm and it is focused on the 'usability trials' that the firm conducted on its product, towards the end of the design phase. Woolgar's central suggestion, based on his experiences, is that the notion of a computer 'user' is being formed in and through the usability trials themselves. Rather than confronting their test subjects with machines and asking them to 'do what they will' with them – inviting them to hack, or tinker – the

---

[2] Feenberg writes of the 'inner tendency of technical development to construct synergistic totalities of natural, human, and technical elements' (1991: 195).

[3] Not least, Feenberg's own observation that 'the capitalist technical code militates against solutions that place workers once again at the centre of the technical system' for their 'human intelligence and skill' (1991: 194).

usability trials are set up in such a way as deliberately to constrain the user and to limit her freedom of action in connection with the machine. Woolgar traces this attempt to constrain the user's actions to the culture of the firm that is making the computer. Within the company, users were talked about in terms that Woolgar compares with overt prejudice, even racism. Stories circulated about how users had abused machines, or screwed up with them in spectacularly stupid ways. The underlying preconception about putative users of the product was that they were uniformly ignorant about computers and how to use them properly (1991: 73). This negative talk about users was '...nearly always couched in terms of insider-outsider contrasts' (1991: 71); the function of the term 'user' from the point of view of company insiders was precisely to maintain a boundary between themselves and the world beyond the organisation.

Consequently, while the norm within the company was for machines to lie around in disarray while technicians dabbled with them at various stages in their construction, when it came to usability trials the computers were placed in cases that concealed their technical innards. This was done to protect the symbolic integrity of the machine and the company. Hence, labels were applied to the cases that warned the subjects of the '...dire consequences of unauthorised boundary transgressions: electrocution, invalidation of the warranty and worse' (1991, 79). It was also done in an effort to conform to the expectations that users were said to have of machines:

> The machine would not be a real machine unless it was in its case. 'Real' in this usage specifically denotes 'the kind of machine a user would expect'. This contrasts markedly with what counts as a real machine within the company. (1991: 76)

Given the presumption of ignorance, the task of turning people into 'real users' – people who could use the machine properly – would require careful attention to how the machine was presented to them, as well as ready availability of manuals and support literature (1991: 80). Through these means, the users were 'configured' by the context created by those responsible for the trials and by the mode of presentation of the machine. Woolgar reports that the users who participated in the trials felt that they were being tested for their ability to use the machine properly, rather than the machine being tested for the affordances it held out to them. His account of the background to the trials makes it clear that, in a very important sense, they were correct to feel this way. The machines were being defined in the course of the trials, with some functions emerging as easier to use, others as less so, and so on. But this definitional process was severely constrained by what the users were *not* allowed to see of the PC and in the course of the trials it was established that '...users have a configured relationship to it, such that only certain forms of access/use are encouraged.' (1991: 89)

It is far from clear that aestheticising the PC interface has any impact on this, essentially exclusionary logic of the hegemonic design process. On the contrary, the attractive and easy-to-use PC comports well with the prevailing ideology that many, perhaps most people are not technically adept, in consequence of which they are actually fearful of overtly technical objects. It certainly does not challenge this assumption. Moreover, the 'friendly' interface enhances control of the labour process through the reified authority of its messages, which provide a series of steps the worker must go through (Murphy *et al* 1986). They also enhance management control by providing a constantly updated source of information on employee productivity. The fact that these interfaces are deliberately contrived to mesh with the structure of employee action in a 'well-behaved' day means that they can also help control the flow of information within an organisation, ensuring that, despite all the rhetoric concerning 'flat hierarchies', some people are kept more knowledgeable than others. A 'war on culture' (see Robson 1998; Dix 1993) within organisations was actively championed by Management Information Systems specialists throughout the 1990s, precisely because networked PCs enable corporations to reduce their reliance upon informal knowledge held by employees. This knowledge, about processes, contacts and 'tricks of the trade' is now held on company databases and codified into routine processes that are policed by the PC interface.

Given these observations, the social evolution of the PC and in particular its interface, stands out as a contradictory process not radically different from other examples of secondary instrumentalisation discussed by Feenberg. While the interface makes the machine more accessible and easier to insert into prevailing social relationships, the relationships in question are themselves not always desirable. The PC is inserted into social arrangements, but only at the price of having its character as computer concealed. Above all, the interface imposes a degree of homogeneity on the human experience of working with a computer that is not necessary and which reflects the interests of systems level forces. The closed interface attempts to reify the PC into something that it is not and to fix it in our experience at what is only a limited stage in its real evolution. At the same time, the interface imposes a block on learning – users are not permitted any longer to dabble with the machine or to 'look under the hood' as Sherry Turkle puts it. The PC in its current state constitutes a political intervention that traverses the fields of technology design and social control, limiting what individuals and social groups will attempt to do with the technology.

Yet this project is inherently contradictory and problematic for a number of reasons. First, it conflicts with the natural human motivation, identified by Jurgen Habermas as our refusal to 'not-learn' (Habermas 1979: 15). Secondly, it conflicts with the reality of the computer as technology and with what we know about the scene of the technical encounter itself, which involves the normal human response to technology, namely, that of experimentation. And finally, the project of closing off computer technology in this way is radically at odds with the peculiarly and inherently open nature of computer technology. The fact that almost 80% of the programming in contemporary Windows systems is dedicated to interface design is a sure sign that social pressures are distorting the development of the technology (Kirkpatrick 2000: 5) – a further cry from the PC pioneer's emphasis on economy and elegance could hardly be imagined. The interface is the product of a set of hegemonic principles within technology design. It dovetails with a system-driven project to establish a broader kind of hegemony – one that stabilises contemporary uses of technology as the 'right' ones and that tries to limit and harness future developments to the perceived needs of dominant social forces. It is a project that over-reaches itself, however, and in some ways runs to ground in the contemporary hacker culture.

Hacking as Thwarted Vocation

'Hacking' denotes a normal reaction to the possibilities presented by the computer. As I have argued in chapter one, the normal human reaction to a technical artefact is to try and identify patterns in its behaviour that will uncover affordances – means with which to amplify the effects of our own instrumental actions on the world. 'Hacking a computer' is often held to describe abnormal intensity of engagement with the machine, but the seeming intensity must often simply reflect the unusual complexity of the computer as a technical artefact – it invites many hypotheses and interaction with it generates numerous intersecting discoveries. When normal people engage with the PC using the minimal technological attitude and applying the folk technological principle that its affordances conform to causal regularities that are knowable in principle, they find that it is extraordinarily open to exploration and discovery. Viewed in this way, it is not abnormal to hack. In fact, it would make more sense to ask why more people do not do it more of the time. The interface, as discussed in this book, would provide part of the answer. The sense that hacking and hackers are in some sense abnormal derives from the original association of the activity with a minority sub-group and also from the attempt to 'normalise' the user-PC relationship. Paul Taylor is certainly correct, then, to argue that 'hacking and computer addiction are not mutually inclusive' (1999: 45) and to point out that the appearance of 'obsessiveness can be put down to the rapidly changing nature of the networked computing context' (1999: 49). Hacking a computer is the hallmark of a vocation in Feenberg's sense:

> In vocation the subject is no longer isolated from objects, but is transformed by its own technical relation to them. This relation exceeds passive contemplation or external manipulation and involves the worker as bodily subject and member of a community in the life of the objects. The idea of vocation or 'way' is an essential dimension of even the most humble technical practices in some traditional cultures, such as the Japanese, but tends to be artificially reserved for professions such as medicine in most industrial societies. (1991: 189-90)

The artificial truncation of vocation in modern, capitalist societies reflects the needs of the system. When the effective and sustainable social employment of a technique requires experts who can be easily identified as such, then social institutions like professions will tend to emerge. This process is functional for society as a whole in the sense just indicated. It is also important to processes of subjective development:

The doer is transformed by its acts: the rifleman... will become a hunter with the corresponding attitudes and dispositions should he pursue such activities professionally. Similarly, the worker in wood becomes a carpenter, the typist at the keyboard a writer and so on. These human attributes of the technical subject define it at the deepest levels, physically, as a person, and as a member of a community of people engaged in similar activities. (Feenberg 1999: 206)

If contemporary hacking is perceived as the activity of strange, socially dysfunctional or even 'sexually inadequate' individuals, this has more to do with the failure of contemporary society to integrate the now quite widespread expertise with PCs into its status systems and into the lives of adept individuals. Indeed, it could plausibly be argued that there is now no such thing as a discrete class of people who could meaningfully be called 'hackers', since we all hack some of the time. As Chandler (1996) points out, the meaning of hacking has changed more than once since the time of the PC pioneers. It is primarily because the vocation to work with computers in a creative and imaginative way is consistently stymied by contemporary social constructions of the technology that hacking is currently constructed as a problematic activity.

According to Sean Cubitt, the development of modern communications networks in the nineteenth century was accompanied by the emergence of a concept of privacy. This idea served to legitimise workers in the industry and played a role in determining their status that was consistent with their economic position as professionals: 'The meanings of privacy were central to ...the emergence of professionalism among communications workers...' (Cubitt 2000: 127). It is not difficult to imagine that, in the absence of such a recognition of their vocation and an appropriate institutionalisation of their professional status, mail workers might have opened mail to steal, or just as gestures of defiance. Such behaviour would be an (inexcusable) response to the failure of lifeworld structures to reflect their role in systems level improvements. This would, inevitably, have had consequences for the self-esteem of the workers and their self-understanding as 'pillars of society'. Institutional recognition of the workers as professionals ensured their compliance with a set of norms that have remained relatively stable through time.

As seen in the previous section, the aestheticising tendencies of contemporary interface design represent an attempt to use computers themselves as the vehicles for a hegemony that seeks to impose a normative structure on the human-computer relationship. As Paul Taylor demonstrates, in the industries in which people, especially young people, who display an especial affinity with computers might be expected to flourish and achieve professional status, standardisation has become the norm:

Computing... has increasingly evolved from [a] ...craft like approach to [a] ...more scientific reliance upon standardised procedures. (1999: 87) The pressures within computing to adopt more rigorous methods of software development have contributed to the marginalisation of the more craft-based hacker-type programmers. (1999: 91)

Within programming and other sectors of the IT industry, the role of creative individuals is increasingly under-valued and pressure is applied to produce software that can be sold, rather than imaginative, efficient and thoroughly tested products. As seen in the last chapter, the computer games industry provides some particularly good illustrations of this. This drive to churn out sub-standard products for eager consumers, waiting to put something onto their expensive hardware, is referred to as the 'software crisis' within the industry. It is almost impossible to produce programs of sufficient quality quickly enough to satisfy demand, and so quality gives way to quantity. Production processes are standardised so that even the most inventive programmers are actually discouraged from practicing their art and obliged to produce code that essentially copies previous projects or is crudely modelled on past experience. Standardisation is driven by the need for systems level efficiency defined, in under-regulated capitalism, in terms of short-term profitability. It is implemented through heightened management control of the production process and through the development of tools that incorporate principles of interface design.

Indeed, the dominant tendency within contemporary computer programming, towards object-oriented design, may be partially explained with reference to these social pressures, since here the programmer relies on an extensive library of pre-determined objects and classes that may be imported and modified. Software engineers increasingly use tools that will create programmed objects for them and implement logical relations between those objects in accordance with pre-coded methods. These programs ease the cognitive burdens on creative people within the industry, but only to increase the amount of code they can churn out and not to free them up to have ideas that might improve products or even make them more secure against hackers. As Kumar points out, this kind of de-skilling keeps labour cheap and it helps explain the endemic levels of staff turn-over and job insecurity within the IT sector as a whole. Describing this process whereby computer technology is repeatedly re-fashioned to de-skill its operatives he concludes that, 'information technology has a greater potential for proletarianisation than for professionalisation.' (1995: 25). Although there seems to have been an increase in the number of professionals in the workforce, associated with informationalisation, Kumar points out that, '...many of these workers are professionals only in name...' (1995: 25) – their status is not reflected in job security, or pay. While traditional professions rely on a constant, if slowly evolving, body of knowledge (consider law or medicine), information technology revolutionises its definition of esteemed knowledge every five or ten years (Kumar 1995:22).

Standardisation in software engineering involves the maximal exploitation of generic solutions – re-hashing previously worked up code to execute new processes. Just as the development of more simple programming languages offended the aesthetic of the early hackers because it took their actions further away from direct interaction with the machine level, so standardisation makes the working life of programmers less interesting and less challenging. An example of this, which highlights the implication of 'friendly' graphical interfaces in regressive social processes is the 'Rational Rose' program.[4] Increasingly an industry standard, Rational Rose allows the programmer to stipulate objects and their properties in a graphical environment and then implements them in code, to be checked over later. Programmers are still required to think through the logical architecture of their programs, but the graphical interface abbreviates the coding process. Using this and other such tools, quite sophisticated programming tasks can be accomplished quickly, without the kind of close attention to detail previously associated with expert programming. As Taylor points out, standardisation, '...has meant that those programmers of a creative but ill-disciplined bent have been increasingly marginalized' (1999: 87). The consequences of this are three-fold. First, it means that more gifted programmers are likely to be unhappy in their work, with the implication that they will be more inclined to misbehave – partly out of sheer boredom and partly to avenge themselves on 'the system'. Secondly, it means that software production goes on under conditions defined by differences of power and social status that are not based on technical skill – anathema to dedicated computer enthusiasts. Thirdly, standardisation of the software development process results in software that is less secure. This, of course, means that systems everywhere are more prone to being hacked by disaffected adepts whose vocation is thwarted by these social circumstances.

Software that is developed with thought and specific attention paid to unexpected security holes that have been discovered in previous programs is more likely to be difficult to hack. Similarly, the good programmer who is free to spend a lot of time going over their work will turn up such holes unexpectedly and take steps to close them. There is no way to standardise these processes. Taylor characterises this situation in terms of what he calls 'the knowledge gap':

> The knowledge gap is rooted in the difference between theoretical concepts and guidelines to security and the 'nitty gritty' of real world computing situations where security weaknesses flourish in the interstices of continually expanding and evolving computer systems. (1999: 79)

Standardisation then results in more 'security holes' and makes for systems that are both accident prone and easy to hack. The conjunction of more security holes and social conditions that make people more likely to hack, results in more hacking activity. This leads to calls for more security, which then feeds into a sense on the part of workers in the software industry (and, we may add, beyond) that they are perceived less as 'social partners', in the contemporary jargon, than as a threat. In short, there is a negative spiral in motion here.

Although hacking is essentially a normal reaction to computer technology and not symptomatic of any kind of dysfunction associated with harmful effects of the technology, it also involves an attitude towards the machine that is inherently

---

[4] Information on this program may be found at:
http://www-306.ibm.com/software/awdtools/developer/rose/.

disrespectful of the interface and its constraints. Silly pictures and irritating messages that limit us to the 'obvious' next step; dialogues with poor simulations of intelligent interlocutors; helpful dogs or paperclips dressed up to look a bit like Einstein – the hacker sees through this nonsense. Hacking a computer dispels the illusion that it is not a machine and embodies an insistence on learning about the rules that really regulate its behaviour. It probes hidden levels of the PC and, if it sees them at all, is disrespectful of the proprietary messages stipulating who can and cannot access a site or piece of software. For the hacking mentality, or temperament, these surface phenomena are distilled down to their mere informational essence. This attitude, however, pitches the hacker against the hegemonic power whose definitions are inscribed into the technology, essentially by way of its interface. In consequence, hacking is 'kynical' – Peter Sloterdijk's term for the subversive strain of cynicism that runs through Western culture.

Kynicism is a 'historical temperament' that traces back to the 'dog philosophy' of Diogenes. Diogenes was the philosopher who lived in a tub and who notoriously bared his arse to the debating parties in the Parthenon. Not for him the cut and thrust of intellectual debate, or sophistry. Diogenes's was a rationality of the body, a subversion of the intellectual order to be effected by alert, humorous and polemical interventions that symbolised disrespect for power. The kynical impulse is one that sees through plausible rationalisations and compelling arguments to their underlying motivations. It does not unmask these by constructing clever arguments of its own, however, so much as by demonstrating the superficiality of its target and opposing to it the concreteness of life itself, embodied in a gesture or a caustic remark. Sloterdijk's thesis opposes the cynical and the kynical as temperaments that have shaped Western history. Cynicism sees through ideas, values and meanings as mere garnish on the operation of power. It is the perspective of the powerful, who will use displays of power and the circulation of ideas to deceive others, but will not be taken in themselves. Kynicism also sees through the deception, but it renounces any interest in power or in using the signs of social prestige for its own purposes. The kynic seeks instead to undermine power through well-timed gestures that poke holes in its cynical machinations.

This distinction casts light on Sherry Turkle's distinction between the hacker and the PC user, discussed above, and on Sean Cubitt's idea, discussed in chapter three, that resistance to the universalising tendencies of contemporary digital aesthetics involves a technical politics aimed at 're-embodiment' (Cubitt 2000: 23-4). Turkle's observation that '...hackers find soul in the machine...' (Turkle 1984: 320) is suggestive of the way in which the hacker is able to extend himself in the machine, rather than being forced back inside himself in the manner of the games player. When the hacker rewrites the code to make a program more efficient or just different, he assumes a kynical orientation, which is disrespectful of the holding power of the interface. To hack is not to escape the grip of the feedback loop entirely, but it is to act on the insight that the interface is an empty illusion, rather than merely to accept the fact and continue 'using' regardless.

For those who self-identify as hackers, three elements define a great 'hack' and each is consistent with the temperament of Sloterdijkian kynicism:

1. Small tricks lead to great effects. Hackers esteem economy of programming input and parsimony in the use of machine resources like memory and processing power, relative to the scale of the effects achieved as output (Taylor 1999: 45-6). This is an instance of the kynical gesture, timed to cause maximum embarrassment to power. It is perhaps most clear when hackers strike at corporate web-sites and rearrange their logos and slogans. Like Diogenes, 'the hacker is a person outside the system who is never excluded by its rules' (Turkle 1984: 234), while his playful attitude towards politics contrasts with the solidaristic 'long haul' that we associate with the traditional left.
2. Hackers esteem technical know-how and admire sophistication in the manipulation of technology. This extends to a degree of intolerance towards non-hackers and 'users', who do not explore beyond the standardised interface. Similarly, Diogenes emphasised living on your wits and thinking against thought, with a kind of disrespect for 'useful' ways of thinking, or using your intelligence to 'get on in life'.
3. Both hackers and kynics are openly parasitic on big systems. The kynical attitude is to say that there is nothing wrong with wealth and indulgence as long as you do not have to work for them. This attitude is reflected in the unembarrassed attitude to wealth of 'successful' hackers (See Freiberger and Swain 1984 on the case of Bill Gates).

If the hacker is an oppositional figure in contemporary computer culture it is in this, kynical sense. The hacker is cheeky, abusive, strategic and amusing. But he is also fundamentally ineffectual and divorced from politics proper as a domain of integration, co-operation and consensus. The hacker is symptomatic, not of the pathological presence of computers, but of a society that has failed to *negotiate* its way towards reliance on networked PC technology and has not created the requisite social structures with which to make sustainable use of it.

Technological Counter-Hegemony

The oppositional significance of hacking was first perceived in the late 1970s and early 1980s. At this time hacking began to be associated with the hippy counter-culture which, in the 1960s, had been straightforwardly anti-technological.[5] Hacking began to be vaguely associated with a challenge to government secrecy and the power of big corporations. The commercial and administrative use of networked computers meant that long-haired technophiles could, in theory,

---

[5] For the relation of early hackers to the hippy counter-culture, see my (2002). For an account of the status of computer technology in the world-view of counter-cultural movements in the 1980s, see Andrew Ross's (1991) *Strange Weather*.

penetrate the information banks of the establishment. In sociological terms, the discourse around hacking at this time is indicative of the emergence of a socio-cultural sub-group centred on the PC as politically desirable technology, as discussed in chapter two. Hacking at this time was still associated with what was described by Steven Levy as the 'hacker ethic'. In essence, this was the refusal to accept the legitimacy of proprietary claims over objects that only existed in and through computer mediated communication. In other words, data which has to be interpreted before it has any meaning significance or value, should be open in principle for anyone to scrutinise. This reflects the hackers' intuition of the machine as a bundle of elements, including data that has not yet been interpreted, or had meaning read into it. The hacker embodies the minimal technological attitude and seeks to control the computer, while the interface user wants to own the environments she encounters, pre-interpreted as 'virtual'.[6]

The phase during which hackers appeared to be in the advance guard of the gentle revolution was short-lived, however.[7] Media representations of hackers began to shift in the late 1980s, with the film *War Games* (1989) being the most often cited example. Cliff Stoll's (1989) *The Cuckoo's Egg* marks the end of the second phase in the development of the hacker as a figure in popular discourse. Stoll's book purports to be an account of his own tracking of a 'computer spy' through a number of networks that connected US security and defence activities to a German anarchist. Viewed in this way, it is a great detective story. However, it actually describes two fundamentally related processes that brought the second phase of 'hacking' to an end. First, the book narrates the conversion of Stoll himself from a fun-loving hippy-type, not unlike the bearded anti-establishment hacker of earlier media representations,[8] to a paranoid, computer world sleuth. Second, there is the growing awareness, which develops throughout the book, of hacking computer networks as a potentially dangerous activity, one with perhaps even life-threatening consequences. Stoll's work marks the beginning of a phase in which the discourse around hacking shifts from being indicative of the presence of a counter-cultural sub-group and begins to speak more of and to the cultural mainstream. The idea of hacking came to signify a new threat to social order and to individual security. As an ever-growing range of socially critical functions were

---

[6] The user temperament involves us in a strange operation, whereby we refuse to look at underlying data structures, even though we know they are there, and persist in committing to an illusory world of light as if it were real, even though (and partly because) we know it is not. This is the cynicism of the gamer, discussed in the last chapter. A good illustration was the recent public auction of an 'unused' Windows folder icon for $17 million on e-bay.com. I am indebted to Jesper Juul for this story.

[7] Levy (1984), Chandler (1996) and Taylor (1999), include a further phase in the history of hacking associated with the development of the computer games industry in the 1980s. I see this as more of an offshoot of the development of a culture of experimentation with the machine which developed throughout the 1970s and 1980s. I am not convinced of the usefulness of the 'games era' as a category in the history of hacking.

[8] Stoll even says at one point that he would 'rather be at a Grateful Dead concert' than tracking down his adversary.

devolved to networked computer technology throughout the 1990s, hacking was increasingly identified as a serious human, commercial and economic problem.

Throughout that decade, the hacker was demonised in the popular press[9] and the once affectionately regarded 'hippy hacker' was displaced by the 'cyber-punk'. The media portrayed hackers as 'nerds'; socially dysfunctional people, who are either criminally motivated in themselves, or may be prone to manipulation by criminals or terrorists. At the same time, however, positive representations of the hacker abound in popular culture. The best example of this is the 1999 movie, *The Matrix*, in which a hacker discovers that reality itself is merely an interface. In hacking his way past it, Neo discovers a horrifying and bleak reality but decides that it is necessary to confront this and to liberate the rest of humanity from its illusion. Read in this way, the film dramatises many of the social conflicts that continue to shape PC and network technology.

I have stressed above the absence of norm-conferring institutions for computer adepts as a causal factor in the genesis of hacking as a problem. Coming at the issue of vocation and professionalism from the other way, so to speak, Andrew Ross traces the widespread concern about hacking to the lack of accountable professionals upon whom ordinary users, can rely. The new generation of professionals who work with computers, seem to be culturally different from those of previous generations. Traditionally, people with responsible and well-paid jobs were thought of as intrinsically ethical, the very definition of good citizens. Moral order and economic power were in some kind of balance. System and lifeworld were effectively integrated with positions of power being embedded in a symbolic pattern that was stable and had popular legitimacy. This has not happened to any discrete strata of people in the computer industry. Ross traces the absence of such an institutional environment to the fact that hackers refused to be 'professionalised', because of their commitment to the freedom of information expressed in the hacker ethic. He interprets this latter as 'a principled attempt... to challenge the tendency to use technology to form information elites' (1991: 84). On this interpretation, the normal link between technical expertise and the hegemony of technological rationality, discussed in chapter one, has been broken, essentially by hackers themselves. This, however, creates anxiety among the population who are obliged to depend on an industry that does not inspire confidence and seems to be fundamentally exploitative, or make themselves vulnerable to the attacks of a group who stand outside the normal technology-society power relation. Demonisation of the 'hacker' works because it is a symbolic projection of our collective anxieties.

Ross argues that the prevalence of the talk and mythology around hacking, which reached its most frenzied pitch in the early 1990s, is also functional for capitalism. The system drives down on 'hackers' and demonises them because this deters people from messing with the systems that they have to work with from day to day. The discourse on hacking is an attempt to uphold the social currency of officially sanctioned expertise. Converting the media image of the hacker from

---

[9] A process described at some length in Taylor (1999).

something cuddly and associated with freedom of information into a dangerous, irresponsible kid who might blow up the world protects the interests of corporations, for whom information is closely linked to power. This reductionist logic is also present in Paul Taylor's thesis that the computer security industry 'labels' hackers in order to marginalize and persecute them. In his account, the media appear as unwitting tools in this process:

> ...the computer security industry uses various rhetorical processes, such as its internal-boundary-forming discourses and its external use of media stigmatisation and symbolic legislation, to marginalise the computer underground... (Taylor 1999: 112-3)

Taylor suggests that the hacking community is subject to a labelling process initiated by computer security professionals and furthered by the mass media. He criticises this as a process of boundary formation and maintenance that serves to exclude hackers from the computer industry by defining them as deviant and 'criminal'. His proposal is that we understand hackers on the traditional 'delinquent' model. The labelling of hackers is instrumental in constituting them as a community of deviants. This actually re-enforces 'negative' behaviours on their part which originate in a sense of exclusion and of having 'no place' in the current order of things. The solution is, of course, to welcome the hacker into the fold and to restore their sense of self-worth by involving them in, for example, the computer security industry.

Much of the current anxiety about hacking can be partly attributed to the changing class nature of individual hackers. Early computer enthusiasts, like Stoll, were essentially middle class and not likely to misbehave; indeed they made the adjustment to professional status with relative ease. During the 1990s this changed as more people from lower middle and working class backgrounds gained (limited) access to machines. Paradoxically, even as it became a source of anxiety for respectable society, hacking also began to be promoted through 'on-line journals' that were read by thousands of people every day. Taylor quotes one of his 'hacker' respondents as saying, of the year 1989:

> In a matter of months the number of self-proclaimed hackers tripled, then quadrupled. You couldn't get through to any of the old bulletin boards any more – the telephone numbers were busy all night long. Even worse, you could delicately work to gain entrance to a system, only to find dozens of novices tromping around the files. (Taylor 1999: 120)

Anyone armed with a networked computer, some instructions and some illicitly obtained passwords[10] could begin to 'hack'. Under these circumstances, although it is true that there are still a few people who are particularly good at hacking, understanding their psychological or ideological peculiarities, if they have any, is unlikely to be key to the sociological explanation of hacking. The disposition to

---

[10] They may of course be guessed. It is well known that most people's passwords are easy to work out and the most common one is 'banana'.

hack, or hacking temperament resides within us all. As Sherry Turkle says, user and hacker are not fixed identities, but ways of responding to the technology that we 'cycle through' in the course of a normal day; they do not denote individuals but states of mind and 'different modes of relationship that one can have with a computer' (Turkle 1996, 32-3). The diffusion of networked PCs has brought with it the social spread of hacking as an attitude and as a practice, while the social conditions described in the previous section serve to make it more likely that people will 'hack'.

In these circumstances it is not appropriate to attach explanatory significance to the ideals of early hackers about freedom of information. Much more significant is the dominant representation of the computer itself. In *The Matrix* the computer screen from which we can view the matrix program contains green symbols against a black background – it is a command line interface. From this perspective, the hero of the film is able to deconstruct the simulated world of experience and to see the truth that those with power do not want him to see. He uses this vision to attack the system from within, through kynical interventions in the matrix itself. Ironically, to defend the lifeworld values of truth and meaning, the hacker must attack through a medium that is austere, difficult and demanding. The system responds with seductive and harmonious images, aimed at withholding technology from any attempt to invest it with alternative meanings or possibilities.

Reality

Hacking must be understood in terms of the social problematics of technology construction. The PC is still 'open' to determination. The situation is unusual because systemic employments of the technology have proceeded in advance of any firm resolution of what the PC or networks are 'for'. In this context, hacking gives us access to a privileged standpoint on the reality of the technology. Those who self-identify as hackers – who embrace this temperament perhaps most of the time that they use PCs – are in the grip of a thwarted vocation. They are experts denied professional status. The proposition that hackers are still contesting the PC is best highlighted by the continued production of 'open source' software that is available over the web. Although most people still prefer to pay money for mass produced software that is substandard but accessible to new users, free equivalents are nearly always available to down-load. Hacker web-sites and shareware distributors publicise information on where to gain access to different kinds of program.

The practice of producing software for free, in keeping with the ethics of the early hackers is best represented by the growth of the Linux operating system. As is well known, this program is an alternative to Windows that has evolved through the collective endeavours of hundreds of hobbyist programmers from around the world. Their efforts have been co-ordinated by Linus Torvalds, a self-proclaimed hacker based in Finland. Torvalds and his peers have created Linux out of love for the technology rather than in the pursuit of profit. This is undeniably an act of rebellion emanating from a minority sub-culture which still serves as a kind of centre of gravity for those who are motivated to dig deeper into their systems. The hacker aesthetic, which I am arguing is of greater explanatory significance than hacker ideals, is also maintained by the open source principle – Linux remains essentially a command line system and the whole idea of closing off the coding levels from scrutiny by users would be completely antithetical to the Linux project.

On the face of it, there is little connection between this high-minded idealism associated with technology and the kind of sneaky prying and stealing that are popularly associated with hackers and the criminal aspects of hacking. I submit, however, that there is a deep connection between the two, which turns on the hacking sensibility discussed earlier – both in its technological orientation and its kynical dimension. There is a clash of perspectives here, which turns on the vantage point one has on the technology itself and the temperament with which one enters the technical relation. Argument about the rights and wrongs of hacking has less to do with ideals in the traditional sense – including ideals invested in the technology – than it has to do with competing perspectives on the technological object itself. Those who want to use computer networks for a productive purpose, related to the pursuit of economic advantage view the technology under completely different descriptions than people do when they have begun to hack code. Taylor understands this in the following way:

> The dispute between the computer security industry and the computer underground as to whether or not it is ethical to break into systems is most often conducted with reference to the analogy of breaking and entering into a building. ...Hackers prefer to compare computer intrusion to being tempted to walk into somebody's house when the door has been left open. (1999: 147)

The argument fails to get us anywhere, Taylor argues, because all such metaphors are 'essentially contestable' (1999: 144) and of the 'ultimate non-transferability of virtual world concepts to the real world' (1999: 133). This conclusion is premature, however, since discussion aimed at reaching agreement is the only way we have to a solution of the hacking problem. Moreover, as I have indicated already, Taylor's view that computer mediated communications require a new language is simply unjustified.

Taylor is not alone in asserting the need to develop a new language with which to discuss 'virtual' objects in computer-generated environments (cf. Johnson 1997: 217). This, however, is surely an illustration of what Espen Aarseth (1997) calls the ideological use of 'industrial terms' – in this case to reject the possibility of consensus on what matters when hackers violate someone else's privacy. The absence of consensus on an issue as important as the normative framework for computer use makes discussion and resolution necessary. To defer this discussion is to effectively renounce any role for reason in mediating the claims and counter claims of computer-mediated technical politics and to hand over determination of such matters as the reality of a computer 'file', the validity of an e-mail 'signature' and the legitimacy of ownership claims in cyberspace to commercial interests. A more pragmatic approach would be to mediate between the various perspectives and to defend positions on these questions that seem to be in the general human interest. What matters in computer mediated interaction is the same as what matters in non-computer mediated interaction, namely, our intentional actions against a background set of shared ontological commitments. At present we do not disagree about the latter, or lack a common way of talking about them. We just vary, according to our perspective, on what the best level of description of the computer world actually is. There is prevarication on all sides too, when it comes to trying to pin the discussion down and this, hackers would be correct to maintain, is a consequence of system players rushing to exploit the networked PC in the absence of a public discourse in which its purposes and limits have been properly agreed.

The dissensus traces back, then, to the sociological issues discussed above. The hacker code of ethics rationalises their activity by insisting that all information should be freely available in principle; that it is folly to put information onto a network if you do not want it to be public; that no pop-up window can assert your territorial right to stop them from probing the networks, and so forth. For the hacker the computer is a kind of 'natural' object crying out to be experimented on and controlled. Standard capitalist theories of initial acquisition, entitlement and rhetoric about 'networked communities' (Stoll 1989: 280) rationalise the activities of the computer security industry. For them, the user mixes her labour with virtual objects and thereby acquires ownership rights that have to be protected. What is contested, however, is not 'virtual territory' but the appropriate way to describe essentially the same activities. The solution to this debate is a discussion aimed at reaching consensus on which descriptions of the networked environment really matter to most people most of the time. This will serve to ground the competing rhetorics in a universally agreed notion of the human interests served by networked computing. On this basis a consensus may be reached concerning the real limits of the technology and what its legitimate uses are. At present, hackers are too engrossed in the non-human levels of description to see the meaning-significance of their own activity for others. Taylor confuses this with an attachment to 'virtuality' which he says blinds the hacker to the reality of the harm they may do to others (1999: 151) – in fact almost the opposite is true. Hackers are not sold on virtual objects at all and this is why they disregard that way of speaking about what goes on in computer networks. The corporations are intent only on exploiting the information processing capacities of the network, without regard for its other uses – as communications medium and as tool for democracy. The latter have embodied their interests in the design hegemony, which focuses on the illusions of 'front end' computing as if these defined the computing experience. The analogy here is with commodification; in capitalist societies one often has the feeling that only the things that can be bought matter. This feeling is false, but it has deep social and psychological roots.

In identifying the appropriate level of description upon which legitimating discussions may converge, we need to start with some notions about what constitutes a good netizen. Only from this starting point will we be able to identify 'virtuous' uses of the web – those that everyone can agree ought to be prioritised –

and to privilege these by ensuring that they are not disadvantaged, legislated against or otherwise inhibited by the machinations of power. Examples might well be the open source movement itself which, after all, holds out the prospect of a technologically enlightened citizenry in control of its own networked destiny.

'Hacktivism' and Technical Politics

Although it is sociologically important to highlight the role of hegemonic design practices and social labelling processes in creating the hacking phenomenon, neither are sufficient to explain public disquiet around the issue. Similarly, it is not sufficient to attribute media representations of hacking to the drive to sustain hegemony or to labelling processes, although both of these play a role. The problem is that hacking really is, or can be, a dangerous activity. Stoll describes, for instance, the operation of computers managed by an associate of his named Chuck. Chuck's computers controlled the directional discharge of ions for use in different scientific and medical contexts:

> By flipping magnets at the right times, Chuck's computers send these [ions] to either a physics experiment or a cancer patient. A bug in the program is bad news for both. The hacker wasn't just poking around a computer. He was playing with someone's brain stem. (1989: 197)

Indeed, the more diffuse it becomes the more hacking imperils the society that places an increasing number of its core activities onto networks that are intrinsically vulnerable, in the absence of a consensus of the kind just discussed. Hackers are themselves not ready participants in such a dialogue.

The social conflicts behind the public discourse on hacking and its dangers centre on a lack of agreement as to what the computer is and what we have to be to make appropriate use of it. The conflicts are complicated by the fact that the technology does not exist in some pristine state waiting to be used. As Feenberg's critical model would suggest, it is already muddied – its true potential is obscured and those best equipped to explore it are locked into social and temperamental positions that render 'objectivity' impossible. Given the diffusion of PCs and networks these conflicts are thoroughly political and centred largely on the design of the technology. This latter will shape the character of social co-existence for most people in the countries of the developed world over the next few decades. Jordan argues that in 'hacktivism', hacking is reconfigured (2002: 121) as a specific manifestation of the 'transgressive' politics that he terms 'activism!'. According to Jordan, hacking is transgressive because it flouts pre-established, hegemonic 'information codes' which regulate what we may legitimately do with information about and held by ourselves and others. These concerns lead hacking to become political, because the system flouts them. However, as argued above, hacking does not need to be 'reconfigured' by hacktivism; it is a moment in technological politics proper and plays a role in contesting the design and use of technological infrastructures that are shaping social life. At the same time, it is also not inherently progressive. The kynical temperament is consistent with undemocratic attitudes towards the technically inept, for instance, and with a kind of individualistic gesture politics that is ineffectual at best. When Jordan invokes 'hacktivism', he intends to mark the association of hacking with so-called 'real world' politics and the new radicalism for which his own work is the totaliser. Hacktivism can contribute to 'activism!' by offering technical tools for other struggles. Less fruitfully, Jordan acknowledges, it may drift into an isolated information-based 'virtual' politics. The dilemma of hacktivism, faced by hackers, is to serve 'real' politics, or to serve themselves on the terrain of cyberspace. The danger of hacktivism is that it may divert struggle into the virtual realm, although as a form of action it holds out the possibility of a second front in any number of conventional political conflicts (2001: 151).

However, as argued here, Jordan's distinction between the real world of politics and the 'virtual' one lacks any purchase because hacking is already a part of the real world of what people do with their machines from day-to-day. The real politics of hacking concerns the relationship between social action and interaction, computer networks and technology design. The dilemma for hackers is of the same kind as that which faces the spontaneist and voluntaristic elements involved in anti-capitalist and other social movements – whether to stand outside the system and assume destructive, kynical postures in relation to it, or to seek a consensus with system players that incorporates their key values of democracy, equality of access and a future based on enlightenment and open communication. The politics of hacking is technological politics, in Feenberg's sense of a struggle between social groups over the control of technical processes. At the heart of democratic technical politics is:

> ...the aim of bringing the social strata located in the post of capital under social control. Socialism would gradually reduce the operational autonomy of managerial and expert personnel and reconstruct the divided and deskilled labor process they command. This new form of struggle... I will call 'technical politics'... (1991: 57)

Hackers contribute to this in the form of alternative technology designs, which prevent consolidation of the hegemonic form of PC design. However, the fact that there are no alternative structures for recognition of their expertise, related to a new public scrutiny of technology, is in part attributable to the kynical stance of hackers.

On the other side, we have a greedy and acquisitive systems sphere that attempts to assert its dominance through technological embodiments of its hegemony – the interface – and through exaggerated campaigns of vilification and heavy handed use of the criminal law. As kynical gesture, the hack is also politically significant in expressing opposition to this. But hacking is potentially threatening, especially to naïve users, and may actually deter others from using, still less experimenting with the technology. The politics of the kynical gesture is, viewed in this way, the politics of failure since it seeks no meaningful alliances and is necessarily unaccountable. It makes consensus on the basic realities harder to achieve by cynically undermining them, just as the cynical predatory practices of capitalist corporations (the monopolistic practices of Microsoft are only the most famous illustration of this tendency). The current sociological and criminological literature is divided on how to address the hacking problem. Stoll's solution is more security. This is a project without end that will only reinforce the negative spiral discussed above. Taylor's is different security – a philosophy and a practice that involves recruiting young hackers early and getting them 'on board' before they are recruited to criminal or terrorist causes. This too leads nowhere – if successful it would result in computers that were completely secure against a non-existent threat. The problem will only be adequately addressed when we establish new structures that institutionalise the professional use of computers and formalise a normative basis for incorporation of the computer into social life. This will only be possible on the basis of a probably unprecedented opening up of technical infrastructures to public understanding and scrutiny, and the emergence of new mechanisms of accountability and legitimation.

Chapter 6

Gaming Publics and Technical Politics

Introduction

According to Andrew Feenberg, we are living in an era that is increasingly defined by social conflicts centred on technology. This is so, not only in the narrow sense that individuals and groups are fighting for access to or control over technological, as distinct from natural resources. It is true in the more interesting sense that social actors contest the design and production of technology in the first place. What Feenberg calls the 'design critique' of technology has been operationalised by human beings with an interest in the form, purpose and social function of technical artefacts. This chapter concludes by drawing further on critical theory and ideas from some classical thinkers on political right to gain insight to the underlying politics of information technology design. Traditionally, critical theory has been suspicious of technology. Reservations about the role of experts in particular and their ability to skew social development in the direction of an oppressive instrumentalism, or an overweening systems sphere, unites all the Twentieth century critical theorists. In the computer age, it seems, the problem of expertise can be tackled. We can opt for 'easy to use' technology that will subvert the hold of experts over technology by facilitating control by ordinary, non-expert individuals. Alternatively, we can change human beings so that they become more technically adept. The former has been the dominant strategy and this has seen a subtle reinsertion of power into the politics of design, with the user friendly interface as a strategy. We need to do both – make technology accessible and make people more adept at using it – if we want to create the technological basis for a more rational way of life.

Critical Theory and Technological Politics

A number of theorists have argued that, in the changed social conditions of the Twenty-first century, the political energies of critical theory need to be re-directed into conflicts that are spatially and temporally more restricted than the grand historical projects of the past. Social activism occurs around issues that are subject to a narrower definition than 'the transition to socialism', for instance. This narrowing of the political field need not mean the same thing as limiting the number of participants; the issues that motivate people and the action they take may be global in scope, but the narrative construction that most people put on them will limit their significance to something short of what, for Lukács (1991) and a generation of thinkers, defined critical theory, namely, its ability to totalise. And just as actions no longer move within a horizon of world-shattering significance, so the coalitions that bring them about lack a relationship to past and future that might guarantee any belief in their permanence ('the workers have always made history') and fold this into the motivational basis of subsequent action ('we will win in the end'). One of the striking things about the 'anti-capitalist movement' of the 1990s, for instance, was its lack of an organisational centre with public structures of accountability, a publicised history, or even an elaborated sense of purpose beyond the immediate goal of bringing various things – events, discussions, systems – to a standstill.

This change in the way that social actors think about their own political endeavours and the ways in which they frame activism in their own lives has been related to the advent of informationalism. Computer mediated communication has transformed the ways in which we communicate and create cultural contexts of action and interaction. The sense that there is no central vantage point from which epistemically privileged agents can grasp the dynamics of the social process as a whole and locate themselves within it has a clear analogy, if not a material explanation, in the diffusion of computer networks. That people rely on the latter to mediate their relationships with others, who may be spatially distant yet emotionally close, and to explore aspects of themselves in the pseudo-anonymity of cyber-space, may well underpin the sense that relationships and inter-personal investments made today can be withdrawn with little cost tomorrow (Giddens 1992). These changed circumstances for political engagement and their technological co-ordinates were theorised in advance by a number of writers. As early as 1989 Felix Guattari, for instance, considered it likely that computer technology would open up numerous possibilities for the formation of political alliances and that this would occur against a background of open-ness and contingency of the kind just alluded to. Referring to the 'phenomenal growth of a computer-aided subjectivity' (1989: 38), he writes:

> In this era of the information revolution... new modalities of subjectification are continually emerging... The information and telematic revolutions are supporting new 'stock exchanges' of value and new collective debate, providing opportunities for the most individual, most singular and most dissensual enterprises. (1989: 62; 65)

From this perspective, the widespread use of computers constitutes an opportunity for 'individual competence' to become a factor in social developments, opening up scope for opportunist interventions that effect small yet important changes in the lives of individuals and societies.

Ulrich Beck, in his *Risk Society* (1992) also traces changes in the spatio-temporal context of political action and the new opportunities that seemed to be emerging to developments in computer technology. For him, a central precept of traditional social theory, namely, the principle that technology evolves in a separate sphere from the rest of society and determines the limiting conditions on initiatives at the level of social planning and culture, is challenged by digital technology:

> ...micro-electronics is introducing a stage of technological development which *refutes technically* the myth of technological determinism. ...computers and control devices are programmable, that is they are functional for the broadest variety of purposes, problems and situations. Thus, technology no longer prescribes how it is to be employed in detail; quite to the contrary, this can and must be fed into the technology. ...One must know what type of social organisation in its horizontal and vertical dimensions one *wants*, in order to use the networking possibilities of electronic control and information technologies at all. (Beck 1992: 216)

For Guattari, Beck and other theorists of this period, the computer is a harbinger of radical possibilities. Their intimations of this reflect the hobbyist and hacker culture that was spreading across Europe in the 1980s and continued into the early 90s. From 1982 to 1986 the Commodore 64 PC dominated this market, superseding the Sinclair Spectrum and out-performing the early Apple Macs. The Commodore was primarily bought as a gaming machine, but many gamers at this time were also keen programmers. As well as buying 'off the shelf' games for their machines, hobbyists would write their own games in BASIC and exchange (or sell) them through hobbyist magazines. More than 17 million Commodores were sold between 1982 and 1993 (Edge 2003). It is probable that most were simply used for playing games. However, the point is that machines like this, which were open to experimentation and allowed users to produce their own programs, were widely available and discussed. As late as 1989, the culture around computing was dynamic and experimental; people exploited the openness of the machines to develop new creative competencies. The early 1990s saw the birth of a 'hacking' counter-culture and of the 'open source' and 'shareware' movement, which made similar, creative use of the Internet (some of these may have been the enterprises Guattari was referring to in the comment above).

The networked computer became a locus for the kind of activity that defines the new radicalism of the 1990s. Hackers and hobbyists made creative use of it to explore new ways of being and of seeing and experiencing the world. In so doing, they began to fashion what is widely thought of as a 'virtual realm' within which new kinds of social interaction became possible. This has facilitated the appearance of on-line communities and associations of people whose primary focus is not the network or the computer but communication. They use the technology to forge alliances and to co-ordinate activities. The 'stop the city' protests of 1999 were, perhaps, the best illustration of this to date, in which technical knowledge, cultural experimentation and social radicalism came together to cause disruptions all over the world but no fixed movement or organisation ensued (Gere 2003; Jordan: 2002).

However, the computer has also been seized upon by more conservative social forces. In the years since 1989, the power of networked computing has been used to restructure core business processes and it plays a leading role in the economics of globalisation. Nearly every small and medium sized business now has at least a dozen PCs and most have their own intranet (Robson 1998). Using the Internet, especially for advertising, is now normal practice for any capitalist firm. Obviously, for computers to have taken on the kind of mainstream presence and function that they have the tendencies just referred to – for people to use computers as experimental playthings with radical social implications – must have been largely neutralised. This has been achieved largely through design of the user interface.

Interface Politics

As mentioned in chapter one, the design of technical artefacts has traditionally been left outside the problematic field of critical social theory. For Marx, technology was in itself essentially neutral with respect to social questions – of justice, exploitation and freedom. To suggest that technology design was already motivated by social and political concerns of a retrogressive nature would have conflicted with the terms of Marx's belief in historical progress. Technology as implemented under capitalist conditions may have regrettable consequences but these flow from what the technology is used for and the manner of its employment. It is legitimate, then, to criticise nuclear weapons as an abuse of the science involved in their design, since they benefit no one and are likely to do great harm to many. It is also reasonable to criticise the deliberate use of technology to increase levels of exploitation in an industry and to make workers' lives less bearable. These lines of critique do not, however, target machines and other artefacts in themselves but the social uses to which they are put and the manner of their employment.

Andrew Feenberg has argued persuasively, however, that there must be a third aspect to any worthwhile critique of technology, which he calls the 'design critique'. This is the idea that, far from being 'neutral', 'technology is a dependent variable in the social system, shaped to a purpose by the dominant class' (Feenberg 1991: 35). Beck's observation above suggests that this likely to be more true of computer technology than of previous kinds, because the computer is a tool that automates *social* processes. It works according to some notion of what the correct social process ought to be, which will be set down in the program. This latter idea of correctness is more obviously problematic than the notion that underpins traditional tool design, which we might summarise as 'maximise productivity and minimise expenditure of labour-time and energy'. Feenberg's critical theory of technology argues that we need criteria with which to assess technological design, relative to agreed social standards.

Automating productive processes that have already been systematised and which present themselves to actors as a kind of reified 'second nature' (Habermas 1992a) may lead to social unrest – if workers are made redundant, for example, but it does not necessarily involve a reflexive reassessment of the purpose of an organisation. However, the impact of using networked computers on modern office work has involved precisely this kind of auto-reflexive shock. The move to 'flat hierarchies' in the late 1990s, for example, was precipitated by the sudden awareness that a lot of what organisations did before computers concerned an information-power nexus that no longer obtained if everyone had access to a networked computer. Since all employees can, in principle, access all relevant information, there is no need for layers of management containing individuals with organisation-specific specialist knowledge. Management Information Systems literature of the later 1990s advocates and records the demise of overpaid 'informal experts' as organisation players (Robson 1998; Dix 1993). The progressive political implications of this levelling out of information access within organisations were to some extent contradicted by the potential use of the networked computer as an industrial spy. As David Burnham (1984) argued, it was as a tool for management command and control of industrial processes that the computer first entered the modern workplace. This is a contradiction because if everyone could potentially know the whereabouts and performance of everyone else in an organisation and, moreover, if everyone was equally able to manipulate or destroy that information then there would be no management gain. Clearly, then, continued use of the computer as a management tool was inconsistent with development of a workplace culture of hobbyistic experimentation and play. Beck notes that with computer technology, '...employees could become transparent for the plants (management)', but also that '...the plants could become "transparent" for the employees and the interested environment' (1992: 218). This last possibility was effectively neutralised by the development of machines with opaque interfaces.

This was not the effect of a management conspiracy but the outcome of a convergence of social factors. Aesthetically, the graphical user interfaces of the Apple Mac and early Windows machines were much more pleasing than command lines typed against black screens encountered even by BASIC programmers. The design principle behind these interfaces is one that promotes immediate access to a range of prescribed functions, rather than inviting experimentation. As seen in chapter three, the individuals who designed the graphical user interface (GUI) saw themselves as wresting control of the machine away from a 'programming elite' and opening up the power of the computer to ordinary people. It is questionable whether it would have been possible, given the level of education and technological training of the population, to have introduced non-'friendly' computers on the scale that Windows has been inserted into every conceivable social location. Although the GUI interface contains built in limitations to what people can do with 'their' machines and filters the information they can access when using them, it also shields them from unwanted information that they would not understand. In so doing, it facilitates communicative and other processes related to the 'non-technical' aspects of activity and work.

The factors just cited count in favour of a less challenging, more opaque interface. They also, however, introduce new and unacknowledged distributions of knowledge and power, with social import. In Beck's terms, the use of networked computing redistributes risks, imposing new risks on the ill-informed. Ignorant use of computers and computer networks exposes people to the negative consequences of hacking, Internet fraud and abuse by experts in authority or working for 'sharp' commercial organisations. If this is generalised to society, the decision to base an increased range of vital functions on the operation of networked computer technology is made without adequate recourse to knowing populations competent to make realistic assessments of the desirability of this. This places computing firmly within that set of risks discussed by Beck, wherein people are increasingly reliant on experts to define the real risks and to protect them from them, while these experts seem to be divided among themselves. The Millenium bug furore was, perhaps, the most high profile illustration of these processes.

Viewed in more Guattarian perspective, the user interface clearly imposes unwarranted limitations on creative activity with computers. Contemporary operating systems contain ever more elaborate means to control what 'users' will do, or even think of doing, with their own machine. The person who buys a machine loaded with 'Windows XP', for example, has (probably inadvertently) purchased a number of 'opportunities' to connect to the Microsoft Network, where, should they attempt to do something not within the predetermined range of the software they have already paid for, they will be encouraged to buy extra software packages. Whether that software could really do the job is another matter, as is the availability of free, functionally equivalent, software for the new task elsewhere on the web. These interfaces inhibit and constrain human beings from finding out about the technical infrastructure they are using. They are accessible and attractive to use, but they are not as friendly as they seem – they offer to help us, but at a price.

The PC interface is a product of conflicting social pressures. Many of the conflicts that have shaped the interface are ongoing and the PC is, perhaps, itself not yet determined in its final form. This makes the elaboration of sociological criteria for good interface design all the more pressing. Feenberg suggests that technology is desirable if it enhances communication and learning processes. As a criteriological standard, this applies most particularly to computers because, for the reasons just discussed, they hold out the possibility of prising technology free from its association with simple productivity maximisation:

> Workers in 'symbolically mediated environments' have very different needs from those in mechanical ones... This sort of activity requires a redefinition of work as a developmental process engaging the worker and his or her capacities as much as the machinery of production. Learning and work merge in this new technical environment. (Feenberg 1991: 95)

As we have already seen, Feenberg's assessment of the user friendly interface is largely positive, precisely because these interfaces facilitate communication and information sharing rather than obliging people to interact with the machine. The reflections above, however, suggest that we need to revise this and add a further criterion for socially responsible interface design, namely, that it holds open the possibility that the user may improve her knowledge and use of the machinic level itself.

This criterion is, perhaps, an instance of Beck's 'reflexive politicisation'. People seem to use computers to communicate and to share information, but if that communication is policed by intelligent programs recording every key strike and facial expression (Garfinkel 2000; Jordan 2002: 123) and the information accessed has been filtered by biased software beforehand, then we need to take these factors into account. The only way people on the ground can get this knowledge is by mastering further, deeper levels of the machine in order to see how their actions have been configured by it. In this sense, the third criterion is necessary – it must have been applied at the design stage – for the other two to have any serious application. All three criteria enable us to situate and comprehend the positions of the various actors involved in the on-going social construction of computer technology. In these micro-politics of user interface design, the hegemonic design is met by two temperaments: the kynical posturing of the 'hacker' and the distinctively cynical play of computer 'gamers'.

As discussed in the last chapter, the hacker is someone who is disrespectful of the rules that are codified into the machine interface and which attempt to regulate the course of their interaction with it. The hacker sees through the interface and knows it to be a cynical mask on the underlying machine. Rather than play along with the choreographed sequences that the interface designer would foist on him, the hacker reaches straight through the lie, into the code and protocols that make it possible. Hackers take pleasure in deriding the naivety of those who accept the metaphoric world at the interface literally. They esteem the cleverness that pulls this veil away and exposes the reality – that what we are given is merely 'window dressing'. At the same time, this is not, for them, a self-consciously 'political' act, in the traditional sense of being concerned with the management of public affairs. It has more to do with a desire to make well-timed gestures that would point up the hypocrisy of those who would use control of technology as a platform for participation in public life, including an overt interest in politics. In all this, hackers and hacking temperament bear a marked affinity with the kynics, followers of the 'dog philosopher' Diogenes, who mocked the 'rational disputations' of other philosophers as mere deceits (and conceits).

The opposed computational temperament to the kynical hacker is that of the cynically compliant game player. The ideal PC user, the reference point for interface designers, does not think about how the machine works when she is using it. She takes for granted that it is able to tell what she wants on the basis of her clicking neatly representative icons. Perhaps she feels that she really is 'dragging' and 'dropping' objects in 'virtual' space. Of course, there is no such thing as the ideal user. After some time at the PC interface, and especially after it has frozen on us a few times, we have started to relate to it as something machinic. We know that if we just grasp the requisite causal regularities we will be able to repeat the task we have just learned over and over. Then we can go home. This is the mind-set of the computer gamer who, having been seduced by the game interface – its characters, its scenery, its music – becomes habituated to the routines that are essential to successful play. In Sloterdijk's history of Western civilization, kynical and rebellious consciousness is opposed by a cynicism that sees through the illusions of power but does nothing to dispel them. Instead, cynical consciousness turns illusions to its own advantage. In Sloterdijk's memorable formulation, 'The cynical gaze lets things know that they do not exist as real objects for it, but only as phenomena and information', but the cynic does not act on this insight (Sloterdijk 1987: 146). So it is with the computer game player. He is aware of the underlying algorithms that guide the game, since they drive his physical movements from moment to moment – his body is colonised by the regularities of the machine. But unlike the hacker he does not re-appropriate himself through application of intellect. The game player succumbs to the meaningless disenchantment of the interface and continues to play regardless of how empty the experience has become.[1]

'Hacktivists'

Hackers are people who have acquired the expertise required to take control of a personal computer and make it do things that are not part of the publicised functionality of specific, pre-packaged software. Hackers understand the technical possibilities of a PC and they gain this understanding by exploring it to its limits. This involves writing their own code in programming language, or changing code in an existing system to make it do things it was not intended to do. The thrill of the hack lies in this getting a machine to do something its designer did not intend. Bruce Sterling cites the case of using a TV remote control to unlock cars fitted with automated alarms as an example of a 'hack' in this, classic sense (Sterling 1992). Hacking a machine requires an experimental attitude, sometimes referred to as lateral thinking and, in the case of computers, intense thought and concentration. The computer hacker refuses the easy way through a computer or a network – the way that is mapped out by the interface – in favour of their own path. This latter course takes them closer to the zeroes and ones, the pulse of electricity that constitutes the physical basis of the virtual world at the computer screen. They have to think in terms of underlying protocols regulating the exchange of data; the programming that defines different systems, and the physical properties of chips and other hardware that affect a computer's performance.

As seen in chapter two, early hackers were esteemed for their abilities with computers and are rightly associated with many of the innovations that have made the spread of computing possible (Weizenbaum 1976). However, the sociological significance of the hacking temperament has changed dramatically with the advent of networked personal computing. This is reflected in media portrayals of the hacker in the 1990s, discussed in the last chapter. The figure of the 'hacker' became detached from a specific group of people or even a sub-culture with its

---

[1] The cynicism of the gamer is the key to the distinctively 'guilt-free' nature of cheating when playing computer games. Entering cheat codes and enjoying their consequences involves a break with the illusion or 'simulation' at the interface, but it does not disturb the coherence of game play.

own ethical codes and the term became a label that could be applied to anyone found guilty of deviant behaviour with networked computers. The hacker label is now charged with both positive and negative connotations – they are super-heroes and nerds. This change in the perception of hackers and hacking reflects their role in the technological politics under consideration here. International computer networks have become the locus of what Beck theorised as a redistribution of risks. Advanced societies have placed a large amount of information on these networks and many information processing tasks with profound human dependencies are carried out using the economies that networking, as distinct from working on isolated PCs, can provide. From the operation of surgical machinery, through offender management in the criminal justice system (Hanley 2003), to air traffic control, networked computers have become pivotal to the operation of numerous strategies of social control. Those who have knowledge of the workings of these systems are frequently not those who operate them from day to day. A community safety officer, for instance, may use a networked system to carry out assessments of the likelihood that a new client will re-offend. She will be led through the process by an interface that asks her to respond to a series of questions about the individual. The program then quantifies over these answers to generate a profile of the individual and the best 'control strategy' for that person. The principles applied recede behind the interface, so that expert management of offenders is based on knowledge held by a criminal justice professional, a networked database and a computer programmer. To be sure, the latter will have worked to specifications provided by the client organisation – in this case, the probation service – but they remain implicated in the play of risks that results.

When the interface 'speaks' it does so with a peculiar authority. Being connected to official criteria and standards and flawlessly implementing them in a way that seems 'scientific' and precise, their presence in such decision-making contexts is likely to over-ride such factors as individual judgement, or intuition about an assessed individual. This may be a desirable thing, depending on your point of view, but the sociological point is that this development opens the system up to new risks, for which society has not, as yet, come up with the requisite management systems. In this example, an individual offender and a criminal justice professional are dependent upon a programmer having got the algorithms right – neither of them are in a position to check this, except with reference to the very body of intuitive knowledge that reliance on the computer system undermines. Systems fail and glitches enter programs affecting their operation. In the networked society, a single key-strike at the wrong point in a sequence could have, and has had, catastrophic consequences for individuals.[2] Traditionally, society has had mechanisms for countering such risks and reassuring people that security can be maintained and that there are systems of redress in case of failure.

---

[2] Garfinkel (2000) gives some striking examples of this in connection with the registration of bad debts and financial services in the United States, where some 40,000 people are denied credit every year because their data shadows have become corrupted through human error or confusion of their identity with someone else's.

Computerisation, however, has proceeded so rapidly and against a background of such dramatic economic upheaval that no one knows any more whom to trust. There are no equivalents in the networked society to the traditional 'professionals', whose status alone gave us reason to believe that they would protect us.

As Giddens (1990) and Beck have both argued, the absence of professions that seem to be based upon stable bodies of knowledge and values, reflected in lifelong career paths for individual practitioners who work independently of money and power on behalf of all private citizens, is related to the endemic insecurity that economists relate to informationalisation (Kumar 1995; Castells 1996). These old professions existed at points where danger was permanent and needed to be countered. The availability of information promoted by advanced communications networks, accompanied by increased public awareness of the powerlessness of professionals in the face of a number of pathological lines of development inscribed in the modernisation process itself, has led to widespread disillusionment with them as a source of protection. Anticipating some kind of institutional response to the changed conditions of the 1990s, Beck writes:

> Where danger becomes normalcy, it assumes permanent institutional form. In that respect, modernisation risks prepare the field for a partial *redistribution of power* – partially retaining the old formal responsibilities, partially expressly alienating them. (1992: 78)

In the networked society, the people most subject to risks are those who lack competence even to comprehend their exposure to them, until it is too late. The real problem here is not technological, but concerns the lack of reliable social mechanisms to accommodate the technology and protect people from the consequences of error. It has, though, had consequences for the design of technology; the user friendly interface can be seen as an attempt to block people's efforts to gain some of the power that is being redistributed over their heads. This is the social context in which computational temperaments take on their full political significance.

In Beck's terms, hackers refuse to remain 'incompetent in matters of their own affliction' (1992: 53). Refusing the lure of the interface, they hack the system and gain access to the knowledge that they need to understand the new risks to which we are all subject in the networked society. This underscores the convergence of hacking with political radicalism in fields unrelated to technology, termed 'hacktivism' by Tim Jordan. It becomes particularly important as the Internet is increasingly used by those with economic power and political-military authority, as web-trawling projects like 'Echelon' – essentially a program that spies on Internet users for the US government (Jordan 2003: 123) – illustrate. When Jordan invokes 'hacktivism', he intends to mark the association of hacking as resistance to the electronic panopticon with so-called 'real world' politics and the new radicalism, anticipated by Guattari, for which his own work is the totaliser:

Hacktivism can be caught between offering technical tools for other struggles or drifting into an isolated information-based virtual politics. The dilemma of hacktivism may be to serve politics, which hacktivists must learn to judge for themselves, or to serve themselves on the terrain of cyberspace. Perhaps hacktivism is either diverting struggle into the virtual realm, or for any politics the virtual realm is perfect. (Jordan 2002: 151)

Here, Jordan adopts the dominant understanding of hacking as essentially solitary, even self-seeking activity and opposes this, in the form of a dilemma, to hacking undertaken for political ends – in support of action being taken by counter-cultural groups with no direct interest in computing. This overlooks the role played by hacking in technological politics, however. The point is that hacking is inherently political, in the sense that it acts upon technology in ways that are socially determinate. It challenges established implementations of computer technology, opens up alternative possibilities (especially through the shareware and open-source movements) and exposes the opaque interface as a controlling and deceitful mechanism.

Hacking facilitates reflexive appropriation of the network itself. It addresses the paradox that a system for information diffusion that has demystified so many other branches of expertise itself remains deliberately opaque and shielded from public scrutiny and scepticism. The significance of hacking propaganda, which insists that networks should be open to all to roam where they please and is at the same time contemptuous of naïve 'users' who lack the wherewithal not to put private information into public places, lies in the fact that it problematises the hold of the friendly interface. The key function of the latter, in this regard, lies in its promulgation of proprietary messages, telling people they cannot access this site or view this file without a password and so on. Hackers challenge the definitional framework that legitimises this and ignore the signs. Since the network is a part of the social and political world and not some 'virtual' add-on, so any action that exposes it to exploration, manipulation and possibly redefinition is political. Convergence of hacking with 'stop the city', animal rights, and other oppositional formations is marginal to an assessment of its true political significance.

This latter is inherently ambiguous. Hackers, by their very existence, oblige everyone to address some of the questions just mooted. But they do not do so by promoting public discourse and debate on the social possibilities of computer technology. It would be more accurate to say that, despite the good intentions of many hackers, they promote anxiety about networks that is probably not conducive to heightened public awareness. The ambivalence in media representations of the hacker reflects a widespread insecurity and a feeling of being menaced, not by an electronic panopticon, nor over-reliance on technology for safety critical functions, but by hackers themselves. The computer security industry is merely the front line of the social forces that express these concerns, and they are legitimate to the extent that they reflect interests that are generalisable to the population as a whole. The hacking sub-culture is directly involved in a technological politics in which social forces contest the networked PC. Hackers represent and embody the knowledge that we all need to have if we are to understand the risks we face as a society that is dependent upon networked technology. At the same time, they symbolise and constitute some of those risks. What is needed is a sociological theorisation of the relationship between so-called 'virtual' experience and the spread of physical computers under determinate social conditions. This relationship involves the two computational temperaments (kynicism/cynicism) and the transitions that we all make as we move between them every day. The aesthetics of life and work with computers is definitive of the social mediation of computer technology and of the on-going social contest over what that technology will be used for, by whom and in what (designed) form.

Unwillingness to contribute to the culture of proliferating proprietary software, implemented through interface restrictions on the user's navigation of virtual space is cited explicitly by Richard Stallman as one of his reasons for wanting to write programs that people can use and exchange freely on the net. In his account of the rationale behind his work, for free, on the GNU operating system kernel, Stallman says:

> The overall purpose, is to give the users freedom by giving them free software they can use and to extend the boundaries of what you can do with entirely free software as far as possible. Because the idea of GNU is to make it possible to do things with their computers without accepting the domination of somebody else. Without letting the owner of software say, 'I won't let you understand how this works; I'm going to keep you hopelessly dependent on me and if you share with your friends, I'll call you a pirate and put you in jail.' (Stallman, quoted in Moody 2001: 20)

However, for all that the hacker culture contributes resources for a material culture that resists colonisation and exploitation by capital, as an oppositional political force it does not hold out the promise that Jordan hopes for. Assessed in terms of principles, the 'hacktivists' possess many of the same inconsistencies as the anarchists of the nineteenth century. 'Property is theft' is the Proudhonist slogan that underpins their attitude towards proprietary software and information in general. But property relations really reside in an agreement of attitudes co-ordinated by common respect for the law and institutions of right. The materiality or 'virtuality' of the thing owned has almost no bearing on this, the fundamental issue at stake in all contested property claims.

Measured in terms of its practical social results, ideologically motivated hacking has had only very trivial consequences apart from the creation of a computer security industry that is very influential and a software industry that is deeply paranoid and 'security conscious'. At the level of product design this has resulted in less trusting software with fewer points of access for the ordinary worker to underlying levels of code. As an intervention in the technological politics of computing, then, hacking as a practice is a blind alley. Hacker culture contains radical strands that are committed to socially progressive ideas and there are examples of hacking technology that are funny, inspiring and emancipatory in potential. Open source software is a valuable resource for the future of computing and will, no doubt, play a key role in the struggles that define and shape the form of personal computing over the next few years. To constitute a progressive force in these technological politics, however, it is necessary to contribute to the building of social relationships around the technology and to foster the development of a critical public. Hackers have not done this, being locked instead in a constant, insularising struggle for mastery over their machines.

Moreover, as hacking has become a more self-conscious and socially diffuse activity it has spawned its own, cynical variant – 'cracking'. Crackers make overt criminal use of their hacking skills, using them for personal material gain or for cruel destructive purposes, such as virus writing. The cynicism in such activities can extend to pseudo-radical posturing. In August 2003, for instance, an Internet worm known as the 'love-san', or 'blaster' virus affected hundreds of thousands of ordinary Internet users. The virus was relatively mild, causing Windows machines to crash every time they logged onto the Internet after a few minutes of use. It also incorporated a denial of service attack capability – harvesting e-mail addresses and using them to mount an e-mail deluge aimed at Microsoft, with messages being sent from all affected machines at a time that was coded into the virus. In the text of the program its authors had written a 'cheeky' message to Bill Gates, urging him to 'stop making money' and 'fix his software'. The cynicism of this posture is obvious since the authors of the virus are clearly not motivated by any desire to improve Microsoft software, except in the singular respect of making its Operating Systems more secure. It is not difficult to think of more creative, equally cheeky uses of their coding abilities. These latter would be less likely to get the virus writers well-paid jobs as computer security specialists, though. As Paul Taylor and others have shown, crackers routinely make the transition into work for the computer security industry, once they have proved their abilities through this kind of casual vandalism (Taylor 1999). With the social diffusion of the hacking temperament, it becomes less kynical and loses its oppositional significance; in a strange dialectic it turns into its opposite – the very badge of cynical conformism.

Gaming Publics

As seen in chapter four, computer games have been deeply implicated in the politics of interface design in two ways. Games are the experimental context in which new ideas about friendly interface design have been tested. Immersive, 'virtual' worlds in which symbol recognition and manipulation are key to successful operation and even pleasurable experience, games have been a kind of testing ground for new ideas on how best to integrate the responsive interface into established structures of recognition and action. Games have also helped generate demand for computers. The example of the Commodore, discussed above, highlights this – the biggest selling PC ever was bought primarily for playing games. A whole range of peripherals, ever-expanding memory and processing capabilities tend to find their first market in the game playing constituency, before they make their way into the broader range of commercial and other applications. The computer game industry is, for these reasons, the most robust within the IT sector. Most importantly, from the standpoint of a design critique of the computer interface, the computer gamer is a kind of cultural testing ground for ideas that will shape the interface of the future. So what is computer game culture?

The computer game seems to be displacing TV and radio from many people's lives as the most salient leisure time pursuit – regular users watch 28% less television than their peers (Wellman & Haythornthwaite 2002: 22). TV and radio were synonymous with the 'culture industry' that was criticised by first generation Frankfurt School theorists. Habermas (1989) summarises this critique in the following terms. TV and radio are capital intensive, so that it was impossible for ordinary people to participate. Moreover, these media were organised to manage public moods and tastes so that the demand side of the economy would constitute a favourable environment for an economy that was reliant on fixed means of production that churned out large quantities of product in a routine fashion. The 'culture industry' (Adorno & Horkheimer 1984) tailors its products to the need of an exhausted working population for relaxation. We can see that all of these things have changed in the networked society. It is cheap to use the Internet. Networked computing has enabled 'just in time' production, obviating the need for demand management. And digital technology is 'interactive' – it requires the active participation of the player (Gere 2002: 80).

Viewed from the standpoint of critical social theory, however, the computer game is an ambivalent cultural form. Within it we can find tendencies that merely extend and deepen the hold of pre-digital mass culture, but also evidence that it has the capacity to promote forms of reflection and engagement that equip people to participate in technological sub-politics. Habermas's criteria for this turn on the idea of learning as a dimension of social evolution:[3]

> Serious involvement with culture produces facility, while the consumption of mass culture leaves no lasting trace; it affords a kind of experience which is not cumulative but regressive. (1989: 166)

Habermas cites Meyersohn's observation that watching lots of TV does not make you any better at doing it. The consumerist society induced a mass psychology of consumption rather than participation. It trained people to seek fulfilment through private pleasures of acquisition and consumption, instead of orientating them to exercise control over their society through collective action.

On the face of it, the computer game embodies the transition from literacy, which is strongly associated with reflection, to a predominantly visual and unthinking experience, akin to what Habermas disparages as 'the techniques of the cartoon' (1989: 168). The importance of literacy was that it enabled people to participate imaginatively in action described by novels and other literary forms that raised questions of ethics relevant to life in the bourgeois world. Trashy mass culture, in contrast, does not promote this kind of thinking. TV and radio reduced people to what Sartre described as 'seriality', or Guattari calls 'mechanisms of empty repetition' (1989: 61) in which people are focused on something but have

---

[3] For clarification of this point, see Kirkpatrick (2003).

no project specific to themselves in connection with it.[4] Early computer games were certainly not tools for reflection in any obvious sense. They absorbed the player in a routine and repetitive action that alarmed some psychologists, who saw it as a form of withdrawal. These are still observable features of most contemporary games, even though the latter are more complex artefacts. Game play involves a kind of surrender to the hold of the interface and, in this sense, games interfaces are laboratories for the production of more stupefying and controlling computers.

The early games – such as Space Invaders, Galaxian, or Joust – trained people for life working with graphical user interfaces in the information society. Their value in terms of the first criterion established above – that of learning about the world beyond technology – is ambiguous. However, these games can be interpreted as analogous to the first periodicals, which Habermas says provided an unreflective way into the bourgeois public sphere simply by providing relevant information (Habermas 1989: 43). It was only with more developed literary forms that the bourgeois pubic became fully self-reflective, drawing on ideas of philosophy and great literature to inform its participation in the public sphere. There are signs that a move towards much greater sophistication, analogous to this, has occurred within the games culture. In modern games, narrative and game play sequences (which retain the rhythmic character of early games in most cases) are skilfully interwoven to produce highly provocative experiences. The finest example of this to date is almost certainly *Grand Theft Auto: Vice City*, which offers the player the opportunity to become a gangster who, through a variety of brutal techniques and a series of violent missions becomes, in the parlance of the game, the man with the 'biggest cojones'. This is hardly a model of good citizenship and the game has attracted criticism – it makes game play out of 'drive by' shooting – but it is also a splendid work of cultural politics. Cars in the game have radio stations that overtly satirise American selfishness, greed and even foreign policy. The police in Vice City are open to bribes and behave like the strongest gang in town, rather than objective law enforcers. Perhaps most significantly of all, game play in *Vice City* very rarely takes on the repetitive empty character it has in other games. The narrative context, which is invariably humorous and cheeky, never quite recedes, even in the most frustrating missions. In this way, the game reverses the usual balance of kynical and cynical temperaments in game play.

Of great significance here too is the transformation, with the rise of the home gaming console and especially the playstation, of the immediate social context of gaming. With the notable exception of 'Pong', the first mass marketed games were single player and most people played them in arcades, where other people were a distraction. Contemporary games are played in the home, however, and

---

[4] 'Capitalistic subjectivity seeks to gain power by controlling and neutralising the maximum number of existential refrains. It is intoxicated with and anaesthetised by a collective feeling of pseudo-eternity.' (Guattari 1989: 50)

ethnographic studies (Wright *et al* 2002) show that people playing games enjoy playing against each other and talking (and laughing) about the experience. Contemporary games consoles are designed to go on-line, so that people can interact with other players from all over the world through the medium of the game. In many parts of the world, this kind of social interaction is already a common public activity, in cyber-cafés. Games culture is communicative and becoming more so. It introduces people to each other through the medium of a dynamic interface that forces disclosure of some aspects of self and concealment of others – in other words, it provides a novel circumstance for social engagement and communication. On-line gaming communities have been a feature of life on the Internet for many years, with LambdaMOO and Everquest being the most famous examples. The idea of a community formed in and concerned primarily with the playing of a game is not without precedent and, at the very least, the on-line version must constitute a kind of civic association. Again, the value of these developments in the context of the Internet as a political medium is, as yet, unclear.

Of decisive significance would be the emergence of a critical discourse aimed at clarifying the value of games as cultural products. If it became sufficiently strong within the gaming culture, such a discourse might refract back onto games production itself and, thereafter, modify interface design. A visit to any newsagents in the UK reveals that about a third of their stands are heaving with magazines about computer games. Sometimes these are aimed at children, but this is by no means true of the majority. Few are, perhaps, as intelligent as *Edge*,[5] which recently distinguished itself by mentioning Adorno in a discussion of the computer game as a cultural form. Criticism both institutionalises the lay opinion on a medium and at the same time educates it. The critic must secure recognition from her audience even while raising its expectations and changing its perspectives. Nevertheless, this is evidence of a critical discourse on the computer game which incorporates diverse perspectives on issues that are relevant to design and to the nature of 'usability' in the context of play. A skeptic might respond to this by pointing to the apparently banal content of many gaming magazines. In them we do not find reflection so much as the kind of 'exchange of preferences' that Habermas identifies (1989: 173) with a thoroughly commodified cultural experience. Columns devoted to the differences between PS2 and X-BOX versions of the same game, or conversations between players on the different speeds of Sonic and Tails might fall into this category. However, a review of the games literature and the few ethnographic studies of group gaming disclose a more critical and elevated form of discourse, shaping our experience of games. Gamers exchange moves and tactics, involving experimentation and innovation that often exceeds anything anticipated by games programmers. Indeed, 'Edge' journalist Steven Poole disparages the 'fight' game genre for lacking this dimension to its game play and, in so doing, he heightens other gamers' awareness of this as a critical standard (Poole 2000: 47).

---

[5] *Edge* magazine has a monthly circulation of 30-40,000 in the UK.

There is plenty of evidence that computer games have the potential to serve as a tool to promote reflection and, as indicated in chapter four, the game is a serious medium worthy of further analysis.[6] The critical culture around gaming is, like the game medium itself, poised between extending mass culture and constituting a cultural platform, equivalent to the eighteenth century world of letters, upon which a new public sphere, appropriate to the networked society, might be constituted. However, the best illustration of the kind of positive cultural politics envisaged here concerns the culture of game modification. Games players write and exchange 'mods' – modifications to games programs that include new twists of storyline and environment – and have succeeded, through this activity, in obliging games producers to leave their source code open for this purpose, something hackers have not yet persuaded the manufacturers of Windows to do. This has been achieved through the market, with astute games manufacturers recognising that there was demand for games with accessible source code, but also through successful negotiation and lobbying. Where hackers confront power dramatically and parade their subversions of the interface order only to be suppressed by power, gamers compromise, negotiate and in their time out of the game world – the time of innovation (Walther 2002) – they effect a gradual re-opening of the technical levels of the machine.

Networked Politics

The technological politics under discussion here are a species of sub-politics. Their immediate sphere of influence is narrow and centres on the character of the experiences that people have with computers. There is, however, good reason to think that computer mediated communications and technologically supported environments are acting as a kind of container within which it is possible to discern the lineaments of a new public sphere. The Internet in particular has been cited as a communications medium that brings people together in a context of equal participation and open debate which mirrors the social conditions that obtained when the first, bourgeois public sphere was formed in the Eighteenth century.[7] From this latter context of discussion, debate and, ultimately, institutional forms of governance, sprang the doctrines of right and legitimating discourses that underpin contemporary notions of property and political practice. A number of commentators have suggested that the Internet could form the basis for structures of global governance in the future. This will give greater significance to the issues

---

[6] A number of digital artists have used games in their work – Suzie Treister, Jean-Paul Bichard – and the whole question of game archiving is giving a practical significance to questions of historiography.

[7] Situating the first public sphere in the Eighteenth century already reveals Habermasian commitments on my part. Critics have suggested that the public sphere actually originates in the popular movements of the seventeenth century. Similarly, this formulation unacceptably idealises the Internet as a paradigm of free and open communication – a charge that is also levelled at Habermas's account of the first public sphere.

under consideration here, concerning the kind of place the global networked society will be.

For critical theory, the decisive issues here are the possibilities that will exist for learning and for free communication aimed at problem resolution through consensus. A crucial, yet largely neglected factor in this is the openness of technology to public exploration, understanding and democratically mediated change. Nicholas Garnham is right to point out that,

> The problem is to construct systems of democratic accountability integrated with media systems of matching scale that occupy the same social space as that over which economic or political decisions will impact. (In Calhoun 1992: 371)

This will only be resolved when we actually have a public who recognise themselves as such in the virtual space of the web and other technologically mediated environments. Hackers and gamers are people who are already at ease in these environments and who identify themselves as participants in them. They differ in the fundamental temperament, or computational aesthetic, they bring to the encounter with the interface. The hacker is insubordinate, intellectual and freedom-oriented. The gamer is submissive, allows himself to be conquered by the rhythm of the machine and is pleasure-seeking. *Ironically, however, it is gaming culture that is likely to produce better citizens in the new public sphere.*

In his theorisation of the public sphere, Habermas observes that its first condition was the existence of a kind of 'cultural platform', from which suitably formed individuals could commence participation. This was the role played historically by the eighteenth century 'world of letters':

> The psychological novel fashioned for the first time the kind of realism that allowed anyone to enter into the literary action as a substitute for his own, to use the relationships between the figures, between the author, the characters and the reader as a substitute for reality. (Habermas 1989: 50)

The rise of a popular literary culture at that time enabled people to participate in imagination in the new 'social' world. The computer game culture equips people in a similar way to participate in what has been theorised as a 'new public sphere' in the world of Internet mediated communication and social relations (See Garnham 2000). Surveys of Internet use show that playing games is an important part of what most people use the Web for when they first become users of the technology, although it tends to decline as a proportion of their on-line activities as they become more experienced users (Wellman & Haythornthwaite 2002: 21).

This is the sociological significance of the 'interactivity' distinctive to playing with a computer. Espen Aarseth provides the most searching interrogation of computer games as textual experiences and shows that what he calls 'cybertexts'[8]

---

[8] It is important to note that, for Aarseth, computer games are only one kind of text that can be analysed from the standpoint of 'cybertext': traditional poems, stories and plays can also be cybertextual if certain conditions are met.

involve user-players in an activity of reading that is neither as rigorously determined by the text as traditional reading, but also does not afford them complete freedom to construct whatever meaning they choose, as in the fantastic projections of those who ideologise the 'virtual' as a radically new arena. On Aarseth's account, using these works involves players in a 'dialectic of searching and finding' (1997: 90), which is characteristic of all game play. Play is distinguished from fictional narrative precisely in that it does not involve the willing suspension of disbelief associated with book reading or theatre going, but instead involves us in testing the game world to find out what its real limitations and affordances are. Writing in particular of text-based adventure games, Aarseth states:

> The adventure game user cannot rely on imagination (and previous experience alone) but must deduce the non-fictive laws of the simulated world by trial and error in order to complete the game. (1997: 50)

Aarseth rejects the term 'interactivity' as a way of describing this to and fro that is profoundly characteristic of all computer games because of its ideological connotations. In the mid-1990s, interactivity was a kind of buzzword, used by the computer industry to hype up the new wave of computer technology – as Aarseth correctly points out, at that time to 'declare a system interactive [was]… to endorse it with a magic power' (1997:48). Aarseth also claims, however, that the term lacks precision and in this I think he is mistaken, not least because his own work does more than any other to clarify exactly what 'interactivity' ought to denote, namely, that special experience of navigating a computer generated environment in such a way as to identify its parameters and behaviours, without breaking with the human interface level and moving to a causal or mathematical interpretation focused on machine elements – the parser, the database etc. What distinguishes the computer game is precisely this movement between freedom, critical use of rationality to discover the truth and ultimate conformity with the demands of physical reality. This universality and the experience of freedom that is central to it ensure that the game is more than just an echo of life in industrial society. It is a testing ground for the nature of freedom under social and historical circumstances defined by networked computing. In itself, this does not constitute orientation towards a public sphere on the part of games players, but recognising oneself as a player of a game is isomorphic with self-recognition in the public sphere. The structure of the game play situation reproduces the classical problematic of politics, as defined by Kant in the eighteenth century: the public see the natural constraints on freedom and work to match the scope of individual freedom of action with the real empirical limits on this, in accordance with moral principles that regulate interpersonal conduct (Kant 1982). To do this in a public sphere mediated by the Internet requires citizens who understand the new medium, particularly the nature of the real and its limits[9] and the norms of behaviour that are evolving there.

Self-narration as a player occurs within a medium that parallels that of the emergent structures of administration and regulation of the new society. Just as the original public sphere paralleled consolidation of the modern state as a 'zone of continuous administration' (Habermas 1989: 24) (pre-modern states were haphazard affairs, marked by local and transitory exercises of power), so Internet society requires a participatory culture. The ambivalence of the Internet, described above, means that it could become an electronic panopticon, in which all of our affairs are recorded and citizens are subsumed under their 'data shadows' (Gordon 1986; Mathieson 1997; Garfinkel 2000). The counter to this is a vibrant culture of 'netizens' who are culturally equipped to address such questions as the rights and wrongs of 'virtual property' (Taylor 1999); regulation of interpersonal conduct in cyber-society; regulation of web content; education and access to resources on the Internet; challenging the role of corporate and public authorities in shaping Internet communications, and exploiting the possibilities for imaginative restructuring of 'cyber-space' in line with aesthetic principles. These issues require a degree of culturation and socialisation with reference to the emergent technologically mediated public sphere and this is what people acquire through games playing. Ironically, the computer game player comes to a non-cynical appreciation of the nature of the computer-supported environment.

The widespread experience of playing with computer games has played an obvious role in facilitating the development of legal frameworks that have begun to develop in this area. Most obviously, games provide robust visualisations of non-physical entities and, in so doing, naturalise the notion that we can meaningfully claim to 'own' a file, or 'sign' an agreement when we perform actions that are remote in space and time. Hackers are, perhaps, in denial about this. The computer game has helped to make computer-mediated-communications feel normal so that e-mails, for example, can now serve as legally binding contracts. The computer interfaces that people use for most commercial and other interaction come loaded with visual imagery – coloured objects, icons, applets – that was first developed for games playing and games technology continues to generate spin-offs that are folded into interface design. In this way, the computer game feeds directly into the feel and form of an emerging new environment for public interaction.

The growing culture of game modification ('modding') and the constant discussion among games players of how to make games better suggests that computer game players are not merely passive recipients of these environments, but actively participate in shaping them. As Andrew MacTavish (2003) shows, game modification involves players directly in the process of re-shaping

---

[9] To take a trivial example, only someone familiar with such environments will know when to pay attention to 'error' messages or what significance to attach to 'access denied' under different circumstances. If these are perceived as natural limitations then freedom may often be needlessly circumscribed.

environments produced by games manufacturers and in a series of disputes with computer game publishers, modders have forced the publishers to soften their proprietary licences to accommodate mods. In this way, game players have imposed their vision of how games should be improved and had their ideas taken up (and sold on) by games companies. This story attests to the idea that the computer game is, in significant respects at least, radically inconsistent with the hollowed out interior of the subject of mass culture. The modifications in question frequently display a kynical character – the most famous one, 'Counter Strike' gives the player the opportunity to assume the role of revolutionary guerrilla ('terrorist') in a game that originally simulated counter-terrorist operations,[10] for example. To be sure, computer game companies are acting out of, fairly cynical, self-interest since the 'flexible' licences (EULAs) allow them, rather than the modders, to exploit the modified game versions for further profit. The important point, however, is that, ironically, gaming culture turns out to be the cultural launching off point and to some extent the site of a constituency of social actors who refuse to be assigned a merely passive role in the networked society. Modders are committed to learning in the standard sense (about games and through the process of interpreting game narratives) and they participate in the equivalent of civic associations within the new mediated social space. And they participate in a process of technological, or reflexive enlightenment too, which equips them for fuller participation in the new public sphere (if that is what it is).

As Aarseth writes, in this new sphere, '...the political relationship between participants is decided by their personal technical expertise...' (1997: 170), as well as more traditional determinants like power and wealth. The significance of gaming culture lies in its pursuit of (often) progressive social and cultural objectives through strategies of negotiation rather than potentially destructive direct action. Taking the hacker perspective enables us to see that, in the evolution of cyber-society, money and power frequently attempt to impose their interpretation of the machinic, physical reality that is the PC. The 'standard' mechanisms of reification, seduction and deceit are used to secure hegemony – to fix a single interpretation of what the machine is for and how it should be used. But the meaning of virtual objects cannot be imposed without agreement any more than they can be (politically) resisted without discussion. Contemporary technical politics centres on finding resolution and agreement. At present an imposed hegemonic ordering faces off against a destructive refusal to participate in the collective shaping of reality.

---

[10] It may not be a coincidence that later games in the same genre routinely include the option for such perspective shifting, including the very ideological 'Black Hawk Down'.

Bibliography

Aarseth, E. (1997) *Cybertext: Perspectives on ergodic literature*, Baltimore: Johns Hopkins Press.

Adorno, T.W. (1966) *Negative Dialectics*, London: Routledge & Kegan Paul.

Adorno, T.W., Horkheimer, M. (1992) *The Dialectic of Enlightenment*, London: Verso.

Baudrillard, J. (1994) *Simulacra and Simulation*, Ann Arbor: University of Michigan Press.

Beck, U. (1992) *Risk Society*, London: Sage.

Bijker, W., Hughes, T.P, Pinch, T. (eds) (1989) *The Social Construction of Technical Systems*, Massachusetts: MIT Press.

Bloch, E., Brecht, B., Adorno, T.W., Lukacs, G. (1979) *Aesthetics & Politics*, London: New Left Books.

Burnham, D. (1984) *The Rise of the Computer State*, London: Weidenfeld & Nicholson.

Butler, R. (1994) *Early Modernism*, Oxford: Clarendon Press.

Caillois, R. (1958) *Man, Play and Games*, Chicago: Illinois University Press.

Calhoun, D. (ed) (1992) *Habermas and the public sphere*, Cambridge: Polity Press.

Callinicos, A. (1989) *Against Post-modernism: A Marxist Critique*, Cambridge: Polity Press.

Carnoy, M., Castells, M., Cohen, S., Cardoso, F.H. (1995) *The New Global Economy in the Information Age*, Pennsylvania: Pennsylvania State University Press.

Castells, M. (1996) *The Rise of the Network Society*, Oxford: Blackwell.

Ceruzzi, P. (2000) *A History of Modern Computing*, London: MIT Press.

Chandler, A. (1996) 'The Changing Definition and Image of Hackers in Popular Discourse', in *International Journal of the Sociology of Law*, Vol. 24.

Cohen, G.A. (1978) *Karl Marx's Theory of History: A Defence*, Oxford: Clarendon.

Coyne, R. (1995) *Designing IT in the Post-Modern Age*, London: MIT Press.

Critser, G (2003) *Fat Land: How Americans became the fattest people on Earth*, London: Allen Lane.

Cubitt, S. (2000) *Digital Aesthetics*, London: Sage.

Davidson, D. (1980) *Inquiries into Truth & Interpretation*, Oxford: Oxford University Press.

Dewey, J. (1997) *Experience & Nature*, Chicago: Open Court.

Dix, A., Finlay, J., Abord, G., Beale, R. (1993) *Human-Computer Interaction*, Hemel Hempstead: Prentice Hall International.

Doctorow, E.L. (1979) *Loon Lake*, London: Picador.

Draper, S.W., Norman, D. (1986) *User-Centred System Design: New perspectives on H-CI*, London: Lawrence Erlbaum Associates.

Duvenage, P. (2003) *Habermas and Aesthetics*, Cambridge: Polity Press.

Edge (2003) #126 'The Mod Scene' Bath: Future Publishing Ltd.

Esteban, J. (1991) 'Habermas on Weber', in *Gnosis* 3(4).

Feenberg, A. (1991) *Critical Theory of Technology*, Oxford: Oxford University Press.

Feenberg, A. (1999) *Questioning Technology*, London: Routledge.

Fitter, M. (1979) 'Towards more "natural" interactive systems', *International Journal of Man-Machine Studies* 11.

Flanagan, M. (2003) *Reload: Re-thinking women and cyberculture*, London: MIT Press.

Freiberger, P., Swaine, M. (1984) *Fire in the Valley: The Making of the Personal Computer*, London: McGraw-Hill.

Gadamer, H-G. (1975) *Truth & Method*, London: Sheed & Ward.

Garfinkel, S. (2000) *Database Nation: The death of privacy in the 21st Century*, Sebastapol CA: O'Reilly Associates.

Garnham, N. (2000) *Emancipation, The Media and Modernity*, Oxford: Oxford University Press.

Gere, C. (2003) *Digital Culture*, London: Reaktion Books.

Giddens, A. (1990) *The Consequences of Modernity*, Cambridge: Polity.

Giddens, A. (1992) *The Transformation of Intimacy: Sexuality, love and eroticism in modern societies*, Cambridge: Polity.

Goggin, J., Newell, G. (2003) *Digital Disability*, Melbourne: Hodder and Stoughton.

Goldberg, A. (ed) (1988) *A History of Personal Workstations*, Reading, Mass.: Addison-Wesley.

Gordon, D. (1990) 'The Electronic Panopticon: A case study of the Development of the National Criminal Records System', *Politics & Society* 15(4).

Gramsci, A. (1971) *Selections From the Prison Notebooks*, London: Lawrence & Wishart.

Greider, W. (1997) *One World Ready Or Not*, London: Allen Lane.

Guattari, F. (1989) *The Three Ecologies*, London: Athlone Press.

Habermas, J. (1979) *Legitimation Crisis*, Cambridge: Polity.

Habermas, J. (1984) *Communication and the Evolution of Society*, Cambridge: Polity.

Habermas, J. (1985) *The Philosophical Discourse of Modernity: Twelve Lectures*, Cambridge: Polity Press.

Habermas, J. (1989) *Structural Transformation of the Public Sphere*, Cambridge: Polity Press.

Habermas, J. (1991) *The Theory of Communicative Action Volume 1: Reason and the Rationalisaton of Society*, Cambridge: Polity Press.

Habermas, J. (1992a) *The Theory of Communicative Action Volume 2: Lifeworld and System: A Critique of Functionalist Reason*, Cambridge: Polity Press.

Habermas, J. (1992b) *Post-metaphysical Thinking*, Cambridge: Polity Press.

Hafner, K., Lyon, M. (1996) *Where Wizards Stay Up Late: the origins of the Internet*, New York: Touchstone.

Hales, M. (1980) *Living Thinkwork*, London: Pluto.

Himanen, P., Castells, M., Torvalds, L. (2001) *The Hacker Ethic and the Spirit of the Information Age*, London: Secker & Warburg.

Huizinga, J. (1950) *Homo Ludens: An essay on the social function of play*, Boston: Beacon Press.

Illich, I. (1979) *De-Schooling Society*, Harmondsworth: Penguin.

Johnson, S. (1997) *Interface Culture: How new technology changes the way we create and communicate*, San Francisco: Basic Books/Harper Collins.

Jordan, T. (2002) *Activism! Direct action, hacktivism and the future of society*, London: Reaktion Books.

Kant, I. (1982) *Political Writings*, edited by W. Reiss, Cambridge: Cambridge University Press.

Kent, S. (2001) *The Ultimate History of Video Games*, Roseville California: Prima.

Kirkpatrick, G. (2000) 'Towards a Critical Sociology of the Computer Interface', in *Imprints*, Vol. 5 No.1 Summer.

Kirkpatrick, G. (2003) 'Evolution or Progress? A (Critical) Defence of Habermas's Theory of Social Development', *Thesis Eleven*, Vol. 72.

Klein, N. (1999) *No Logo*, London: Flamingo.

Kline, S., Dyer-Witheford, N., de Peuter, G. (2003) *Digital Play*, Ottawa: McGill-Queen's University Press.

Kumar, K. (1995) *From Post-Industrial to Post-Modern Society: New Theories of the Contemporary World*, Oxford: Blackwell.

Laurel, B. (1993) *Computers as Theatre*, London: Addison-Wesley.

Laurel, B. (ed) (1990) *Art of Human-Computer Interface Design*, Massachusetts: Addison-Wesley.

Law, J. (ed) (1991) *A Sociology of Monsters: essays on power, technology and domination*, Sociological Review Monograph 38, London: Routledge.

Levy, S. (1984) *Hackers: heroes of the computer revolution*, Harmondsworth: Penguin.

Lukacs, G. (1991) *History and Class Consciousness*, London: Merlin Press.

Lunn, E. (1986) *Marxism and Modernism: An essay on aesthetics and politics*, London: Verso.

MacTavish, A. (2003) 'Game Mod(ifying) Theory: The cultural contradictions of computer game modding', unpublished manuscript.

Manovich, L. (2001) *The Language of New Media*, London: MIT Press.

Marcuse, H. (1964) *One Dimensional Man*, London: Routledge & Kegan Paul.

Mathieson, T. (1997) 'The Viewer Society: Michel Foucault's panopticon revisited', *Theoretical Criminology* 12(1).

Metropolis, N., Howlett, J., Rota, G-C. (1980) *A History of Computers in the Twentieth Century*, New York: Academic Press.

Moody, G. (2001) *Rebel Code*, Harmondsworth: Penguin.

Murphy, J.W., Micknnas, A., Pilotta, J.P. (1986) *The Underside of High-Tech: Technology and the Deformation of Human Sensibilities*, New York: Greenwood Press.

Negroponte, N. (1995) *Being Digital*, London: Coronet.

Nelson, T. (1990) 'The Right Way to Think About Software Design', in Laurel (1990).

Nickerson, R.S. (1976) 'On conversational interaction with computers', *Proceedings of the ACM/SIGGRAPH workshop October 14th-15th, Pittsburgh*.

Nielsen, J. (1995) *Multimedia and Hypertext: The Internet and beyond*, London: Academic Press.

Noble, D. (1984) *Forces of Production: A social history of automation*, New York: Knopf.

Norman, D.A., Draper, S.W. (1986) *User-centred System Design: New perspectives on Human-Computer Interaction*, London: Lawrence Erlbaum Associates.

Perelman, M. (1999) *Class Warfare in the Information Age*, New York: St Martin's Press.

Pfaffenberger, B. (1988) 'The social meaning of the Personal Computer, or why the Personal Computer Revolution was no Revolution', in *Anthropology Quarterly* 61.

Poole, S. (2000) *Trigger Happy: the inner life of video games*, London: 4th Estate.

Postman, N. (1985) *The Disappearance of Childhood*, New York: Vintage Press.

Preece, J., Rogers, Y., Sharp, H., Benyon, D., Holland, S., Carey, T. (1998) *Human Computer Interaction*, London: Addison Wesley.

Quine, W.V.O. (1960) *Word & Object*, Massachusetts: MIT Press.

Raymond, E. (1999) *The Cathedral and the Bazaar: Musings on Linux and Open Source by an Accidental Revolutionary*, Sebastopol, California: O'Reilly & Associates.

Robson, W. (1998) *Management Information Systems*, London: Pitman Press.

Roszack, T. (1968) *The Making of a Counter-Culture: Reflections on the Technocratic Society and Its Youthful Opposition*, London: Faber & Faber.

Schneiderman, B. (1997) *Designing the User Interface: Strategies for effective H-CI*, London: Addison Wesley

Sloterdijk, P. (1987) *Critique of Cynical Reason*, Minnesota: University of Minnesota Press.

Sterling, B. (1992) *The Hacker Crackdown: Law and Disorder on the Electronic Frontier*, Harmondsworth: Penguin.

Stoll, C. (1989) *The Cuckoo's Egg*, London: Bodley Head.

Sutton-Smith, B. (1986) *Toys as Culture*, New York: Gardner Press.

Sypher, W. (1962) *Loss of the Self In Modern Literature and Art*, New York: Random House.

Taylor, P.A. (1999) *Hackers: crime in the digital sublime*, London: Routledge.

Turkle, S. (1984) *The Second Self: Computers and the Human Spirit*, London: Granada.

Turkle, S. (1996) *Life on the Screen: Identity in the age of the Internet*, London: Weidenfeld & Nicholson.

Walther, Bo Kampmann (2003) 'Playing and Gaming: Reflections and Classifications', in *Game Studies*, Volume 3, issue 1.

Weber, M. (1974) *The Protestant Ethic and the Spirit of Capitalism*, London: Unwin University Books.

Weizenbaum, J. (1976) *Computer Power and Human Reason*, London: MIT Press.

Wellman, B., Haythornthwaite, C. (eds) (2002) *The Internet in Everyday Life*, Oxford: Blackwell.

Winograd, T., Flores, F. (1986) *Understanding Computers and Cognition: A new foundation for design*, New Jersey: Ablex.

Woolgar, S. (1992) 'Configuring the user: the case of usability trials', in Law, J. (ed) *A Sociology of Monsters: Essays on power, technology and domination*, Sociological Review Monograph 38, London: Routledge.

Wright, T., Boria, E., Breidenback, P. (2002) 'Creative Player Actions in FPS Online Video Games: Playing counter-strike', *Computer Game Studies* 2(2).

Zizek, S. (2000) 'From Urvater to Holocaust... And Back', in *Parallax*, Vol. 6 No.2.

Index